THE *Maori* COOKBOOK

HarperCollins*Publishers New Zealand*

First published 1996
HarperCollinsPublishers (New Zealand) Limited
P.O. Box 1, Auckland

ISBN 1 86950 224 8

Cover: food styling and photography
by Stephen Robinson;
food prepared by Lindsay Neill
Illustrations by Helen Casey
Designed and typeset by Graeme Leather
Printed by GP Print

Contents

Introduction   v

The hangi   1

Maori bread   11

Forest foods   15

Seaweeds   22

Vegetables   24

Birds   43

Pork   46

Shellfish   48

Koura (Crayfish)   90

Whitebait   94

Tuna Heke (Eels)   97

Fish   103

Index   133

Introduction

If there is one aspect of my life that I couldn't imagine living without it is food. The bond, especially with kai from home, borders on worship — a heavenly sweet surrender to my stomach. I've tasted many gastronomic sensations around the world, but few compare to the flavours of Aotearoa that I carry as memories on my taste buds. I recall sitting down to a meal of mussels in Brussels — their speciality. I was visiting the city with a delegation of Maori film makers and we were more than just a little curious about their kaimoana; after all, we all shared memories about our own seafood sizzling on open fires back home. I was insulted when the bowl of steaming mussels lying in a garlic and onion sauce was placed in front of me. Not because of the sauce — that was delicious — but because of the size of the shellfish. I couldn't believe that they would be allowed to serve such tiny morsels! Surely this was illegal, just as in New Zealand. but no, I was assured that smaller means sweeter, so I plunged into my miniature, but legitimate, meal. I'd no sooner taken the treat into my mouth than it was gone. It just wasn't a patch on the soft, sweet, monstrous mussels of home, and I told them so!

When I was young I didn't appreciate how lucky I was to be born here. I didn't even think about it when I was sitting on a white sandy beach, cooking up a feed of freshly gathered mussels. Now, though, I remember those long hot summers when my parents would wade out knee deep into the water to pluck kaimoana from the sea. The bounty of kina, paua, cockles, mussels, tuatua, pipi and periwinkles were placed on a makeshift table. We kids would haul big stones together and arrange them in a circle. We'd throw on a piece of corrugated iron that we'd brought with us, light a fire underneath it and wait for dinner to arrive. It was a crude stove by any standard, but whether it was the fresh salt air mixing with the catch of the day, or the old iron trapping the seawater so effectively, it was perfect for our purposes. Personally, I think kaimoana is best eaten this way — plump, spitting seafood, salt-seared by the open fire. We were so spoilt. One year all we had was paua: paua au naturel, paua fritters, paua soup, garlic paua steaks, and even paua soufflé. I was heartily sick of paua by the end of that year, and yet now I mourn the loss of our harvests. I always thought that my child would grow up eating his kai as I had, straight from the sea to his stomach.

Unfortunately, I can't claim to be as enthusiastic about hangi food. In fact, my grandmother once said that I surely couldn't be a real Maori when I refused to eat meat pulled freshly steaming from the earth. I was going through a vegetarian phase, something my relatives felt should surely be put on hold, given the event. But to me, it was not so much the food of a hangi but the sense of occasion it inspired in us all. A hangi was always put down for any big family gathering, and with twenty aunts and uncles on my father's side alone, there were plenty of these. Two of my uncles, Jimmy and Bobo, would play their guitars, my grandmother would sit and watch her children mix and mingle, and I'd study the hangi, wondering how that mound of damp earth was doing its work. The hangi usually came up as the sun went down. Then, as the air cooled the hangi would be opened and the wonderful aromas would blast out. The men would haul the baskets up onto trestle tables and the women would dish the food out. It was the most well balanced, nutritious meal we'd eat in a year. Steamed meat, chicken, fish and plenty of vegetables were overloaded onto our plates. Eating the meal created its own music: the beautiful noise of meat bones being sucked, cabbage slurped, and fish bones being plucked from flesh. Not to mention the crackling bonfire, the guitars, and the singing.

I also recollect looking out of the kitchen window one day when I was about eleven, and seeing my father scaling our cabbage tree, knife in hand. I thought he must be pruning it, but instead he brought its sweet, soft centre into the house, and boiled it up. My mother wouldn't let us anywhere near it, saying she'd tried it once and it was much too sour to inflict on developing and impressionable taste buds. I longed to know what brought my father such joy, and later in life I was to find out. I was offered a dish from a crowded hui table one night and, without a second thought, munched in to this stringy, bitter-flavoured substance. This was my introduction to kouka, and once I'd mixed it with a little puha and meat I was hooked. Unfortunately, all my attempts to grow cabbage trees at my home have failed, and occasionally I look longingly at my neighbours' trees, harbouring deep, satisfying memories of that delicious meal.

My affection for food must be obvious by now. In fact, if it wasn't for an iron will I would be the size of a house. The first time I tasted rewena bread and fried bread I was in heaven. The rewena's distinctive tangy bite accompanied by watercress, ham and some nice gruyere was all I needed to convince me that this was a bread I should steer clear of, lest I make it my only meal from that point on. Fried bread I cannot resist. As soon as I see it on a table at any marae I literally fall on it like a hungry dog, devouring as much as my stomach can bear.

My father often did the cooking when I was young, especially on the weekends. He would boil up silverside, watercress and dumplings, and if we were really lucky he'd follow this up with some fried bread. His dough was the softest in creation, and even now when I go to make a batch I can't figure out how all his pummelling and pulling made his dough so light and fluffy when it was fried. My family would sit around the open fire watching television and buttering up these huge breads. I would insist that mine was piping hot so the butter would melt the instant it hit the bread, and then I'd dribble on golden syrup. Just writing about this is making my mouth water so once I've finished here I'll say goodbye to all my good intentions, give in to my childhood desires, and find comfort in the Maori food from home.

Joanna Paul
August 1996

The Hangi

Blue New Zealand skies, warm summer nights and summer holidays — it's time for a hangi. As the smell of cooked food rises in the evening air, we can celebrate with the traditional Maori way of cooking food.

METHOD

1. First, select your site. When choosing the location for your hangi, there are a few things you will need to bear in mind:

- You will need access to water for soaking bags and cloths, and creating steam.

- Make sure the soil is easy to dig. Also, arrange to dig your hole in a piece of wasteland rather than in somebody's lawn. If the hole must be dug in a lawn, remove the top layer of grass and put it back afterwards.

- Be aware of the direction and strength of the wind. Keep a watchful eye on your fire, and make sure it is sited well away from buildings, trees or anything which may catch a flying spark.

1

Make sure it is at least 3 m away from the nearest object and nowhere near any overhead obstructions.

- If food is to be consumed outside, the site will have to be located in an area where the participants can mingle and eat without discomfort.

2. Secondly, make a list of all the food items you will want. All varieties of meat, fish, poultry, vegetables and steam pudding can be cooked in a hangi. Typical things to cook include sides of meat (mutton, beef, pork), poultry (chicken wrapped in foil), potatoes (two per person), kumara (one or two per person), pumpkin (one serving per person), taro, carrots, marrows, chokos, onions, butternuts. Cabbages and green vegetables are better cooked in other ways, not in the hangi. Prepare the food in the same way as if you were going to cook it on an electric stove, then put it in containers; these should be placed within easy reach of the hangi before the pit is cleaned out.

3. Thirdly, make a list of all the materials you will need. This should include the following items:

- STONES. When heated the stones will supply the heat for cooking the food, so it is important to choose stones that do not crumble or shatter when heated. The best stones to use are those that have been tried by the local people. Igneous (volcanic) rocks are better than metamorphic or sedimentary (e.g. sandstone) rocks. There are several types of suitable rock:

  Auckland Bluestone — this is a hard, brittle, blue-black rock.

  Riverhead Rock — this can be obtained from Kawakawa Bay and Dargaville. Selecting the right rocks requires some skill: they should be round, loaf-sized stones, and should make a high-pitched ringing sound when struck with a hammer.

Volcanic Rock — this is the type of rock used during the Depression to make stone walls. It is good rock to use, as it heats quickly, doesn't throw out chips and is light to handle.

Fire bricks — some people today use a combination of fire bricks with the stones mentioned above, but this is not a recommended practice.

The number of stones necessary will depend on the type and size of stone selected. For a hangi feeding up to 75 people, you will need enough stones to fill a hole approximately 0.5 m deep, tapering in diameter from about 1 m at the top to 0.75 m at the bottom. The stones must be thoroughly dried out before use.

- FIREWOOD. Aside from newspaper and kindling for starting the fire, you will also need timber for burning. For a successful hangi you will need a mixture of dry timber and slow-burning logs. Hardwoods are better than softwoods, as they give out more heat, although lighter timber underneath will help maintain the fire. Suitable timbers include manuka (white tea tree), kanuka (red tea tree), and puriri, although this must be dry. You will need about 45 pieces of wood approximately 1 m long and 5–8 cm wide.

- FOOD BASKETS. Containers can range from elaborately welded, perforated steel canisters to simple mutton cloths. For special dishes where the use of wines or other 'trimmings' is intended, the food can be wrapped in foil. Steam puddings can be put into mutton cloths.

  Baskets can be made from small-mesh chicken netting by cutting a square and folding the corners up. Remember to allow for sides when you are working out the size of the basket. Good sized baskets are 33 cm² (for the large basket) and 22 cm² (for the smaller ones). (Alternatively, wire breadbaskets can be used, if obtainable.)

Depending upon what you serve and how many people you want to feed, you will probably need about three food baskets or containers — one large basket for meat, and two smaller baskets, one for kumara and potatoes, and another for other vegetables. Don't put all your vegetables in one basket.

If the food is to be served from a kitchen, the potatoes and kumara should be placed in one large basket. If the food is to be served from tables outside, several smaller baskets, depending on the number of tables, will prove more convenient.

- COVERING. Two types of covering are needed — cotton and sacking. White cotton is used to cover the food and the sides of the baskets before they are put in the hole. A much heavier covering is needed to keep the soil from getting into the food once the food has been put on the heated rocks. You will need three pieces of sacking or canvas for this; one to lay over the food and down the sides of the basket, and one for each end of the hole, so that soil can't go down the sides. Before this heavy cover goes over the food, it must be thoroughly soaked — this is very important! (The Maori way of cooking uses steam, while most Pacific Islanders roast the food dry.)

- OTHER EQUIPMENT. You will also need: three long-handled shovels, a file, a sharpening stone, mutton cloth, pitchforks, buckets, an axe, a saw, a hatchet, carving boards, a cleaver, knives, forks, serving plates, newspaper (to lay the prepared vegetables on while waiting for the fire to burn down), aluminium foil, aprons, 6–10 tea towels, a wash basin, soap, towels, fly spray, one or more trestle tables (if serving outside), wire cutters, 9–12 sugar bags or sacks, and a hose pipe.

4. Hangi take a long time to prepare, so do everything possible the day before: prepare the meat and vegetables, place wood and stones by the site, and make the baskets. On the day, you will need to be organised in order to have a successful hangi. The chart below gives a guide to the schedule you will have to follow.

Noon	Check gear; exchange courtesies.
1.00 p.m.	Dig hole; lay fire and stones; prepare vegetables and meat.
2.15 p.m.	Light fire.
3.15 p.m.	Have vegetables ready; sacks and other cloths soaked; water should be handy. Seal meat.
3.30 p.m	Place food on stones; cover. Stand by.
5.30 p.m.	Arrange serving area.
6.00 p.m.	Open hangi and serve.

When all the preliminary preparations have been done, you can begin the hangi proper by digging the hole. The size of the hole depends on the size of the food basket(s). Put the basket(s) on the ground and mark out the area around them, leaving at least 10 cm of clearance around the outside edges of the basket(s).

The depth of the pit is largely determined by the number of stones used. It should only be as deep as is necessary to accommodate the stones and yet leave them slightly more than flush with the earth's surface. If the pit is too deep, the soil from the side will taint the food. If the pit is too shallow, more soil than is necessary will be needed to cover the food.

You don't need a very deep hole, either — cooking is just as quick and efficient if a hangi bin is used. This is a large, round, bottomless cylinder (it can be part of a metal or wooden washing machine tub)

5

0.75 m in diameter and about 0.60 m deep, with a close fitting, deep lid to retain the heat and cover the part above ground. (If you do use a hangi bin, though, you must still cover it with wet sacks and soil or turf.)

Once you've dug the pit crumple single sheets of newspaper and put them in the hole. Save one double piece and roll it up like a wick. Put it in the hole near one edge (you will need this to light the paper after you have put in the wood and rocks). Put the kindling in, then start building a pyre by putting on the bigger pieces of wood. Once the wood has reached ground level, it must be stacked in a special way. The woodstack above the ground should be built over the pit by placing alternate layers of wood at right angles to the layer below it. Lay the pieces of wood side by side across the top of the hole, leaving a 1 cm gap between each piece until the hole is covered. On top of this layer put another row, laying it at right angles to the wood below. As the pyre is being erected, the stones should be placed in three or four layers at regular intervals throughout it in a pyramid shape. Build the fire very solidly. It has to burn for an hour or so without being replenished, so must have plenty of body.

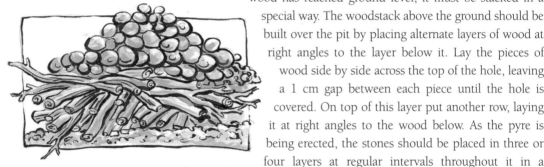

Light the newspaper wick. Keep a constant, watchful eye on your fire. The rocks will begin to change colour when they are hot (the volcanic rock will go nearly white). Before long the wood will burn down and the heated rocks fall into the hole. As the pyre burns down, replenish it with more wood, and return any displaced stones to it (remember, the stones will need to give out heat for two to three hours). After the fire has been burning for an hour, fill the food baskets, arranging the bottom layer carefully. Place the two smaller baskets inside or on top of the larger basket. Sprinkle salt over the food and cover with the white cotton cloth. Put the food baskets near the hole. Now check that the wet sacking is near the hole.

After an hour and a half (or two and a half hours if it's a really big hangi) the pit should be covered in ashes and stones, as the fire has burnt through. At this stage clean the pit. If the pit is not cleaned properly, the ash will spread through the hangi when the water is applied to create steam. (Few guests like the smoky taste of meat cooked with the embers left in the hole.) Remove all the unburnt pieces of wood, raking the hot rocks to one side of the hole with a long-handled shovel. Because of the heat at this stage, some workers protect their head and shoulders with wet towels, and their legs with gumboots stuffed with cabbage leaves!

Make a flat bed out of the rocks, and throw about two handfuls of cold water on to them. The jet of steam will carry the ash away. The stones should then be left laying on the embers. Using a pitchfork, for the heat is intense, place the raw meat on the stones to singe. As each piece 'browns' it is put on a tray until all the meat has been treated in the same way. *This should be done as quickly as possible to conserve the heat.*

When this is completed, your large basket should be placed on the stones. The base should be covered with cabbage leaves, and the partly cooked meat placed on top of the leaves. If the meat is in large pieces it can be placed in direct contact with the stones to ensure it will cook.

Place the vegetable containers on top of the meat in the centre of the hot rocks, while the special dishes and steam puddings in tin foil and mutton bags, respectively, are placed on top of the vegetables. Throw several quarts of water over the food and stones to produce clouds of steam. At this point you need to move fast. Make sure the white cotton

covering is wet, be it cheesecloth, mutton cloth or an old tablecloth. Place layers of this wet cloth over the food to keep the steam in. It is essential to start from the base of the food pile and spread the cloth to ensure the soil does not come into contact with the food. The cloth must cover all the food in the hangi. A layer of wet sugar bags and sacks are used to cover the cloth. Again, the sacks should be thoroughly soaked, and again the covering should begin at the bottom of the food pile, with one sack being placed over each end, then one covering the centre. Throughout the covering process, water should be sprinkled onto the hangi to create steam. It cannot be emphasised enough how important it is to act quickly during this process. It is also very important that the sacks you use have not contained chemicals. Once the cloths and sacks have been placed over the food, the soil is spread on top, forming a dome shaped mound. Again, cover the hangi from the edges, working towards the centre of the mound. Watch for any steam escaping and cover the cracks.

Assembling the hangi should take about 15–20 minutes, and then you can have some well-deserved liquid refreshment.

Leave the food to cook for 2–3 hours before digging it out to serve. (A smaller hangi will take even less time.) Food can rarely be overcooked. A small hangi (for 10–20 people) will take two hours to cook; a hangi for up to 100 people will take two and a half hours. (For numbers of people above these, it is preferable to make two hangi, one for meat and one for vegetables, because the vegetables

Soil

Wet cloths and sacks

Vegetable baskets

Meat baskets

Hot stones

cook more quickly. Allow two hours for the vegetables, two and a half hours for the meat.)

Peel the soil off the hangi from the top to the bottom and do likewise with the sacks and cloth. If steam emerges from the hangi after the first shovelful of soil is removed, the hangi will be successful. If no steam appears, cover it up and buy fish and chips.

Oven Hangi

If you don't want to go to all the trouble of preparing a traditional hangi, or if you simply want something a bit smaller, you can always make an oven hangi. To do this successfully you must have a roasting dish with a close-fitting lid. Pre-heat the oven to 180°C. Sprinkle some parsley and a few pieces of diced celery into the roasting dish. Lay in a few pork bones, and on these place four pork chops (chicken can be added or used in place of pork chops). Add four pieces of pumpkin and four potatoes. Over this lay enough cabbage for four people and, if possible, some watercress. Add 1½ cups water. No salt is needed. Cover the dish and bake 3½ hours. Serves four.

Maori Bread

PARAOA TAKAKAU (VERSION 1)

    1 cup flour   5 Tblsp lukewarm water
    Pinch salt

Mix all ingredients together, knead well and roll out thinly. Put onto a hot floured tray. Cook in a very hot oven, about 200°C. Best served with butter and eaten while hot.

PARAOA TAKAKAU (VERSION 2)

    2 cups flour   Pinch salt
    Water or milk   Baking powder, optional

Mix all ingredients together to a sticky consistency, and shape with as little handling as possible into an oblong 20 x 10 cm. Either place in a tin and bake at 200°C, or wrap in tin foil and throw into fire embers; if cooked in the embers remove the burnt crust before eating. Best served with butter and eaten while hot.

Takakau

5 cups flour
5 tsp baking powder
600 ml milk

Mix all ingredients together and knead very gently. Roll to a flat circle and cut through gently in a cross. Bake on a hot, floured tray at 200°C. Real takakau has no rising agent, just flour and water.

Camp-Oven Bread

4 cups flour
1 tsp salt
4 tsp baking powder
Milk

Sieve all ingredients and mix to a soft dough with milk. Turn on to a floured surface and knead lightly, forming into a ball of dough. Press out into a round 25–30 cm across. Cut through centre both ways into four pieces. Bake in a hot oven 15–20 minutes.

REWENA (Leavening for Maori Bread)

Original Starter:

3 slices potato

2 cups flour

1 tsp sugar

Boil potato slices in 1 cup water to mashing consistency. Cool. When lukewarm, add remaining ingredients and mix to a fairly firm texture. Add more warm water if required. Cover and leave in a warm place to prove.

Starter Plant:

Take 1 Tblsp of dough from the rewena original starter and put into a jar. Feed one day with 1/2 cup warm, unsalted, potato water, and the next day with 1 tsp sugar. Continue alternate daily feeds. Use this as leaven for the rewena bread recipes.

PARAOA PARAI (Fried Bread)

2 cups flour

1/2 cup rewena

Pinch salt

1 tsp sugar

Lard for frying

Combine all ingredients well and mix with warm water to a scone mixture. Flatten into round shapes. Fry in lard and serve with honey or golden syrup.

Paraoa Koa

1 kg plain flour

1 tsp salt

500 ml milk

50 g fresh yeast

120 g butter

120 g caster sugar

4 eggs, beaten

300 g currants *or* sultanas, cleaned

100 g candied peel, finely chopped, optional

Sift flour and salt into a bowl. Warm milk to blood heat (37°C), and add the yeast and butter. Stir until yeast is dissolved, then mix in the sugar and eggs. Make a well in the flour, pour in the liquid ingredients and beat until smooth. Turn dough onto a floured board, work in the currants or sultanas, and candied peel, if using. Knead dough until it is elastic, then place it in a warmed, greased bowl.

Sprinkle the dough with extra flour and cover with a clean tea towel. Set dough to rise in a warm place for 1½ hours or until it has doubled in bulk, then knock down dough and leave to rise again for another 30 minutes. Shape the dough into four small loaves. Arrange the loaves in greased baking tins and leave to prove until twice their size. Bake for approximately 1 hour at 160°C.

Forest Foods

RAUPO BREAD

Describing the method of preparing this food in the 1840s, the Reverend Taylor declared:

'The process of making bread from the pua, or pollen of the raupo is curious, both on account of the patience required to collect sufficient for the purpose, and for religious rites connected with it; showing most clearly, how very much pinched for food the aborigines formerly were, and the great stress they laid upon religion in aiding their efforts to procure it. It is also remarkable for the number of words belonging to the process, which is a proof of the value put upon this article of food.

'The first thing which was done, was the erection of a shed near the swamp, from which the pollen (pua) was to be collected. The process of gathering it always commenced at daybreak; for when the sun began to shine, the feathery seeds blew about, they had then to discontinue their work until the evening, when they recommenced the work. The gathering of the flower heads of the raupo was continued for several

> The Maori utilised an impressive variety of vegetable food gathered from the forest including roots, piths, leaves, fruit and berries, though the food value of these items varied considerably.

days, until a sufficient quantity of pollen was obtained. They then cut a quantity of flowers of the kakako, which being strewed on the floor of the shed, the pua was heaped upon them. It was daily carried into the sun to dry and again returned in the evening to the shed, lest it should become damp with the dew. Parties of from fifty to sixty men, women and children, often assembled for this work; each family having its own division (tuakoi) of the shed to attend to. When the process of collecting was finished, they went into the forest to procure the bark of the hinau, which they stripped off the trees in large pieces, twelve to fourteen feet long. These were doubled up so as to make a bag, one end being left open to form a mouth, while the sides were sewed with flax, leaving only a small hole at one of the lower corners. Being set on their ends, they formed long bags, almost as tall as a man, which were propped up by poles. They then took the mats (tapaki), which had been previously plaited by the women of split flax and spread them on the ground by the side of the bag (pu), part of them stripped the flower from the stem: this process was called uhu. A quantity being shred, it was put into bags, which had been plaited with great care of finely split flax, so as to allow only the smallest particles to escape. Men only were allowed to sift the pua, which was done by shaking these bags over the mouth of the large one, while the tohunga, or priest, repeated a karakia. 'The principal person of each family had to sift it; but, if he had been guilty of any crime, the pua would fly up in his face and he would be forced to give place to a better man. Whilst some were sifting, others were plaiting small baskets (rourou, kapukapa, paro) of green flax, which are lined with leaves of the rangiora or pukapuka, to place the sifted pua in; the siftings (tutae papapa), or down, being thrown away. The plug having been removed from the bottom corner of the bag, the pua flowed out, which was caught in the baskets, carefully avoiding to press it down, in which state it resembled small seeds. The baskets being filled, they were covered over with leaves as before and then sewed up (runa), which being done, they were placed in the ovens (hangi), the number of which was proportioned to the quantity to be cooked. The ovens, having been covered over as usual, were left till the steam burst out at the top, which was a sign that they were done. When taken out, the substance still retained its resemblance to seeds; but the baking converted it into a solid mass.

'The principal person of the party then divided them among the people. Some of the loaves thus made were from six to eight inches in diameter and thick in proportion. The smaller ones were generally eaten at the time, the larger ones being reserved as presents, for state occasions, or for supplies during war. A loaf of seven inches in diameter was sufficient to satisfy two full-grown men.

'Having been rendered sacred by the prayers of the tohunga, or priest, during the process of sifting, no one could eat of it until the first oven, containing only three or four baskets, had been cooked for the priest, who then took off the tapu.

'It is remarkable, that when the down (hune) obtained from the raupo head is put into the baskets, it is invariably filled with a small kind of worm, or grub, in very large quantities. It is therefore, generally baked, and it is at once fit for making beds and pillows, for which purpose it is commonly used, and forms a good substitute for feathers.'

PUA

Shake as much yellow pollen from the raupo heads as is required; add ½ cup water to every 500 g of pollen. Mix, put into a greased bowl and steam for about 2 hours. (The Maori used to wrap the raupo leaves around the mixture and steam it in the hangi.) This tastes just like ordinary bread.

HINAU

The hinau is found in lower forests from the North Cape to Dunedin and grows to about 18 m. The damson plum-like fruits are purple and about 1.5 cm in length, but are not palatable when eaten raw. When they are ripe they fall to the ground (January–February) and are then collected, pounded in a mortar with a pestle to separate the pulp from the hard seeds, which are then thrown away, and the mealy portion is formed into large cakes. Alternatively, hinau berries can be soaked in water for a month or so then sun-dried. The Maori rubbed these between their hands to separate the flowery part of the skin (pulp) from the kernels. The cakes made from the pulp were traditionally cooked in a hangi, but as they harden as they cool, it was quite an art to cook them for the correct time. If overcooked, they become too hard to eat.

The Reverend Richard Taylor, in Te Ika-a-Maui. New Zealand and its Inhabitants *(1855) wrote of the ancient method:*

'To make bread of the hinau, the berries are steeped for nearly a year in running water, to get rid of their bitter and astringent quality, they are then put into a basket (pu) which has been plaited very close, and beaten upon a stone with a small wooden club. This being sufficiently done they are sifted through closely plaited baskets; the husks, thus separated from the pulp, are thrown away, and the latter, which resembles dark flour, is kneaded into cakes with a little water. These being wrapped up in leaves of the rangiora, are placed in a native oven. When cooked, they have much the appearance of very brown bread and are highly esteemed by the natives, though too oily to suit the taste of most Europeans. Hence the proverb which is used by a man when he is waked out of his sleep to eat: "Kia wakaoho koe i taku moe, ko te Watutureiarua" — "When you disturb my sleep, let it be on account of the arrival of te Watutureiarua", the first person who made bread from the hinau.

'The natives sometimes cooked it by pouring a quantity of the flour into water which had been heated by putting hot stones into it, the only way the natives previously had of heating water. In that state it was called rerepi.'

KARAKA

The karaka is a handsome tree between 9 and 15 m high, with dark green, glossy, laurel-like foliage. It grows in coastal forest throughout the North Island and north of the line from Banks Peninsula to Westport in the South Island. The karaka has a prolific crop of berries. This oval fruit, about the size of a plum, is orange when ripe (January–February). The outer fleshy part has an agreeable taste when ripe, but the important part is the kernel inside. The kernels are poisonous if eaten raw, but the Maori used them as food once they had been thoroughly prepared. They have an unusual but pleasant flavour.

Before they can be eaten the ripe berries that have fallen from the tree are gathered from the ground. In earlier times the kernels were collected in baskets and trodden with bare feet in water to work off the outer fleshy part, before being baked in a hangi for 24 hours and stored in baskets. To minimise preparation time it is advisable to select those berries which have lost most of the rich, deep orange outer flesh. Flesh-covered seeds still need to have their protective covering removed by rubbing or peeling.

Rub or peel off any flesh left on the seeds. Place the berries in a container and cover with cold water. Boil for 3–4 hours to destroy the enzyme which acts on an alkaloid called karakine and releases prussic acid. Remove the kernels from the cooker and place in a container. Cover with cold water and steep for a week. The kernels are then ready to eat. Cut the kernel at one end while peeling with one continuous strip to the opposite end of the seed.

FOR LONG KEEPING:

Remove the nuts from the steeping container and spread out to dry in the sun. When thoroughly dry, store in a sugar bag or basket and hang in a cool, well ventilated place.

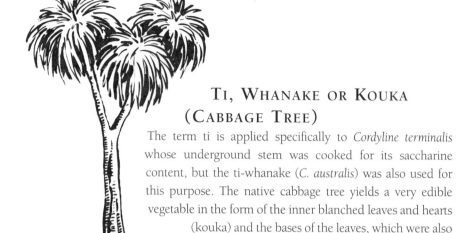

TI, WHANAKE OR KOUKA (CABBAGE TREE)

The term ti is applied specifically to *Cordyline terminalis* whose underground stem was cooked for its saccharine content, but the ti-whanake (*C. australis*) was also used for this purpose. The native cabbage tree yields a very edible vegetable in the form of the inner blanched leaves and hearts (kouka) and the bases of the leaves, which were also eaten raw by the Maori as a green vegetable.

KOUKA (version 1)

Break out the heart of the tree, not the bloom, and strip away the leaves or grass, to reveal a firm white core. Boil in salted water until tender. This is slightly bitter, but is delicious with roast meat.

KOUKA (version 2)

Collect the cabbage tree centres when not in flower — select large ones — and strip all the outer leaves off, leaving the white centre piece. Cook for 30 minutes with puha and serve with corned beef or pork.

TI-TREE SALAD

Open the green bulb on the ti tree and pull away all the outer leaves. Use only the white core, and this, sliced very finely, makes a delicious salad when served with French dressing.

Tupakihi, Tutu, Pukou

Tupakihi, commonly called tutu or 'toot', is a small, rather flimsy tree or shrub with shining soft leaves with distinctive parallel veins and long clusters of purplish, very juicy berries. It grows on the margin of lowland and mountain forests throughout New Zealand, usually beside riverbeds and streams. In September and October, the flowers hang in 1 cm long racemes from the leaf stems, which change from greenish-red to purple in March. The floral envelope then becomes swollen and succulent and encases the purple berry. The green shoots, seeds, stem and leaves are extremely poisonous, even the smallest amounts causing paralysis and death, but the fleshy part surrounding the seeds (the petals) and the juice from the berries are safe to consume, and were used as a food and drink by the Maori. A bowl of tutu juice boiled with the pith of the pitau fern tree was considered a very palatable dish. Juice of the tutu was boiled or fermented with the bull kelp seaweed (rimurapa) to make a jelly.

Seaweeds

PARENGO, KARENGO OR MAKAUE

Parengo is a name given to seaweeds of the genus *Porphyra* that grow in silky reddish or purplish sheets or ribbons between tidemarks. It is also known as 'sea lettuce' in some parts of the country. Parengo is closely related to edible seaweeds of Britain (laver) and Japan (nori) and is considered a delicacy by East Coast Maori. The seaweed is gathered from July to September at low tide and is then sun-dried by hanging on a piece of netting. When dry shake out the sand and store the seaweed.

In the old days, the Maori used to tao parengo, i.e. steam it in a hangi. Today, people are more likely to take a handful of dried seaweed and steam it for 1 hour using 2 to 3 cups of stock and 1 Tblsp butter.

Alternatively, gather young parengo, wash and crush into 2 to 3 cups of boiling water. Add salt and a good heaped tablespoon of butter or dripping and boil for 20–30 minutes. Drain and serve like cabbage. It may also be cooked with corned beef or some rashers of bacon.

Sea Lettuce Hash

Gather sufficient sea lettuce and wash it in cold water to get rid of the salt. Boil in water for 30–45 minutes and add a knob of butter. Salt to taste after draining and serve with bread and butter.

Rimurapa

Rimurapa, the common bull kelp, was often dried by the Maori and used as a food. It has a solid trunk 39–75 cm long and several centimetres thick, and a leathery frond often 39–75 cm wide at its base. It was mixed with the expressed juice of the tupakihi or tree-tutin and boiled to give it consistency, when it formed into a jelly.

Vegetables

KUMARA

KAO (SWEETMEAT)

Kao was a traditional Maori delicacy, made in the autumn after gathering the kumara crop (March–May).

Sharpen a manuka stick for use as a scraper. Select small, elongated kumara-tubers and scrape out the accretions of earth in the hollows ('eyes') on the surface of the tubers. Remove the outer skin carefully, without damaging the inner skin which clings closely to the flesh. Wash the kumara, then wrap them individually in the leaves of the kumara vine or puriri tree, and place in a slow earth oven for 24 hours. Remove the baked kumara and dry them in the sun for about two weeks. The kumara kao is then ready for eating.

Kumara Kotero (version 1)

Take three large, rotting kumara, skin, and squeeze the juice from them until a floury substance is left. Knead into this 1 Tblsp of sugar and a knob of butter. Flatten out into small cakes and bake for 30 minutes in a medium oven. Leave on a tray to cool.

Kumara Kotero (version 2)

Mash some fermented kumara and add 2 Tblsp of flour, cornflour or arrowroot. Season to taste with salt and pepper. Shape into croquets and cook in ashes (the traditional way) or fry in oil.

Kumara Pie

1.5 kg kumara	Pineapple juice and rings *or* chunks
Butter	1/2 tsp cinnamon
2 eggs, beaten	2 tsp brown sugar

Boil the kumara, mash with butter and eggs, and add the pineapple juice and cinnamon. Place in a fireproof dish and decorate with pineapple rings or chunks; sprinkle with brown sugar. Cook for 30 minutes in a moderate oven.

Kumara Chowder

700 g kumara

3 onions, sliced

30 g butter

850 ml milk

450 g tin cream-style sweet corn

Salt and pepper

Whipped cream

Parsley, chopped

Peel and dice the kumara; cook in boiling, salted water until tender. Meanwhile, fry the sliced onions in the butter until tender. Drain the water from the kumara, mash well and combine with the milk. Add fried onion and sweet corn and bring slowly to the boil. The consistency should be thick, but a little extra milk may be added if wished. Add salt and pepper to taste. Just before serving, garnish with whipped cream and sprinkle with chopped parsley.

Kumara and Apricots

250 g dried apricots
2 large kumara
Salt
1 Tblsp sugar
1 Tblsp butter
½ cup breadcrumbs

Soak apricots according to directions on packet. Cut kumara into rounds and boil for 20 minutes. Strain. Place alternate layers of kumara and apricots into an ovenproof dish. When dish is half full, add salt, sugar, butter and a little liquid from the kumara. Sprinkle top with breadcrumbs. Cook in a cool–moderate oven for about 1 hour until the flavours are blended. Serve hot as a vegetable dish.

Candied Kumara

2 large kumara
⅛ cup brown sugar
1 tsp bacon dripping
¼ tsp nutmeg

Peel kumara and boil for 15 minutes. Drain kumara, split lengthwise and place in a roasting dish. Combine all other ingredients and boil until sugar is dissolved. Pour over kumara and bake in a moderate oven for 10 minutes, turning after 5 minutes.

Pork, Apple and Kumara Casserole

8 pork chops	1½ cups cooked apples
2 onions, sliced	*or* 1 tin sliced apple
1 Tblsp chopped parsley	3 Tblsp lemon juice
½ tsp mixed herbs	2 Tblsp sugar
Salt and pepper	Kumara, peeled
2 cups tomato juice or soup	

Pre-heat oven to 180–200°C. Deep-fry pork chops in frying pan for 15 minutes. Remove and place in casserole dish. Cover with onions, chopped parsley, mixed herbs, salt, pepper and tomato juice or soup. Cover and cook for 20 minutes. Combine apple, lemon juice and sugar, bring to boil and place on top of casserole. Place kumara on top of the apple layer and cook with lid off for a further 30–60 minutes.

Kumara Crumbed Roll

Kumara	Mustard powder
500 g veal, finely minced	1 egg, beaten
Salt and pepper	Breadcrumbs

Boil kumara until tender; mash and mix with the finely minced veal and a little fat from some cooked onions; season with salt, pepper and a little dry mustard. Mix together well, form a thick roll, brush over with beaten egg and sprinkle with breadcrumbs. Bake in a hot oven for 45 minutes. Serve hot with green vegetables and chutney.

Oriental Kumara Rissoles

Kumara, boiled

Any leftover vegetables

3 rashers bacon

1 onion

Salt and pepper

1 egg, beaten

Breadcrumbs

Mash kumara and add the other vegetables, such as peas or carrots. Mince the bacon and onion and add to the kumara mix (with a little finely chopped parsley, if desired). Add seasoning, and half the beaten egg. Use remaining egg to coat each rissole before dipping into breadcrumbs. Fry in hot fat, and serve with tomato or plum sauce.

Kumara Loaf

500 g kumara

500 g finely minced steak

1 medium onion, chopped

1 egg, beaten

Salt and pepper

Breadcrumbs

Boil kumara and mash. Combine with the mince, onion, egg, salt and pepper. Shape into a loaf, roll in breadcrumbs and bake in greased loaf tin in hot oven for 45 minutes.

FAVOURITE BROWN STEW WITH KUMARA TOPPING

¼ cup flour

1 tsp monosodium glutamate

½ tsp salt

⅛ tsp ginger

1 kg stewing beef, cubed

Oil for shallow frying

2½ cups tomato juice

12 small carrots

500 g small onions *or* onion rings

500 g small potatoes

Heat oven to 180°C. Combine flour, glutamate, salt and ginger in a paper bag. Shake the meat in this mixture to coat it well, then fry it in hot oil, until brown on all sides. Transfer the meat to a casserole dish, and add the remaining flour in the bag to the oil; cook for 1 minute. Slowly stir in tomato juice, then add this mixture to the meat. Cover and bake for 1 hour. Add vegetables, cover and bake a further 30 minutes at 200°C.

Sweet Potato Poi

2 cups kumara, grated
$^1/_3$ cup raw coconut, grated
1 tsp salt

Mix kumara and coconut together. Add seasoning. Line a small casserole dish with buttered tin foil. Put mixture in foil and fold over to seal. Bake at 180°C for 1 hour. Serve hot or cold.

Roroi (Maori Pudding)

Here is a recipe for what is perhaps the only Maori pudding known.

Take some very fresh kumara, straight from the garden, if possible. Wash thoroughly, then grate. Place in a shallow baking dish and sprinkle with sugar. Over the top of the grated kumara place some broad slices of kumara. This will keep the mixture from hardening in the oven. Bake for an hour at 180°C. When hot this is similar to a steamed pudding, and may be served with cream, or custard. When cold it may be sliced like bread, and spread with butter.

POTATOES

PAKEKE

Take 6 large potatoes, peel, grate and put into a cloth and wring the juice out of them. Add finely chopped onions, and salt and pepper to taste. Shape into patty cakes and fry in peanut oil until cooked. These are delicious served with meat or with pineapple rings. The juice wrung from the potatoes can be used to make arrowroot sauce for puddings.

POTATO SOUP

6 medium size potatoes, grated

2 medium carrots, grated

2 medium *or* 1 large onion, chopped finely

2 leaves silver beet

1 Tblsp butter

1.5 litres milk

1 Tblsp parsley, chopped

Put vegetables in large pot with a small cup water; add butter. Put on heat, stir until thick, and simmer for 10 minutes. Add milk, and bring to near boil. Pour into tureen and garnish with parsley. For a really delicious flavour, add 150 ml cream just before serving.

Pumpkin

Pumpkin Soup

450 g pumpkin	Bread
600 ml milk	30 g butter
Sugar	

Cut pumpkin into small pieces and cook in salted
water. Rub through a fine sieve with the liquid, then add
the heated milk in order to give the soup a creamy consistency.
Season and add a little sugar. Put some fairly thick slices of bread
in the soup and simmer gently for 6 minutes. Remove from heat,
add butter and pour into a soup tureen.

Pumpkin Cake

½ cup butter	1 tsp cinnamon
1½ cups sugar	½ tsp cloves
2 eggs	¼ tsp salt
2 cups flour	1 cup cooked pumpkin
1 tsp baking powder	1 cup raisins
½ tsp baking soda	½ cup nuts, optional

Cream butter and sugar till light, add eggs. Sift all dry
ingredients together three times, add to creamed mixture
alternately with pumpkin. Add raisins and nuts if using. Bake in
moderate oven 50–60 minutes. Ice if desired, or serve plain or
with whipped cream.

CORN

MAIZE WITH WOOD ASH (A BREAKFAST DISH)

Take two cobs of well matured and thoroughly dried maize (the poultry type). Remove kernels from cob and place in a large saucepan (on cooking the kernels swell). Cover liberally with cold water. Bring to boil and allow to boil gently until the kernels swell sufficiently to split the outside horny covering. (It is often necessary to add water to the corn while cooking as a certain amount of moisture is lost in the cooking.) While the corn is cooking prepare the wood ash. Burn the wood of your choice in a clean container so that only ash remains. Make sure that the wood you use is clean and is not contaminated with pesticides, paint, or other chemicals. Once the kernels have swollen to their utmost and are tender, add prepared wood ash.

Stir the mixture well and allow to cook gently for 1 hour or so. It will boil like a hot pool. Remove container and contents from fire and rinse cooked kernels in a kit (colander) with plenty of cold water. Most of the horny husks will come away during this stage.

Place corn back in pot, cover with cold water and bring to boil. Cook gently for another hour, then it will be ready to serve. Serve with cream or milk. The wood ash gives the corn a delicate flavour all of its own.

Baking soda can be used instead of wood ash. In pre-European days, when open fire cooking was a feature of the Maori way of life, the fire place was treated with utmost care and respect. Nothing, absolutely nothing, was burnt in it other than wood.

KAANGA

Quite soon after the Maori acquired the potato, pumpkin and corn, they learned to steep maize cobs in running water until they were partly decomposed, and from this they made a kind of porridge called kaanga. It has a very unpleasant smell to European senses, but is still liked by many Maori today.

KAANGA WAI (CURED CORN)

Shell white corn, place in a flour bag and stand in clean running water for two months. Alternatively, place in a clean tin or drum containing fresh water; change the water daily for two months. Test the corn by pressing it; when it is soft, it is ready for use.

Take 2 cups of preserved corn, clean and mash or mince it. Bring 6 cups of water to the boil in a saucepan and add the crushed corn, stirring all the time. Simmer on a medium element for 1 hour and serve with cream and sugar to taste.

DRIED KAANGA WAI

Put raw preserved corn through a mincer, squeeze out all the surplus juice and leave to dry on an oven rack or in the sun. When perfectly dry, put into bags and store until required.

Take 1 cup of this prepared cornmeal, add to 3 cups boiling water and cook for 30 minutes. Serve with cream and sugar.

KAANGA WARU

Grate corn from the cob. The corn should be just hardening (over-ripe). Add salt and pepper, or sugar if preferred. Put into muslin or corn leaves. Boil or steam about 1 hour and serve.

SCRAPED KAANGA PUDDING

Finely grate ordinary maize (on the cob is best). Add sufficient water to bind the meal; add sugar and/or spice if desired. Form the dough into cakes or rolls and wrap these in corn leaves. Put into boiling water and boil for 2½ hours. This mixture can also be boiled in a cloth like plum pudding. It is delicious hot or cold, cut in slices and buttered.

KAANGA WAI CUSTARD

1 egg, beaten	1 cup cooked kaanga wai
1 Tblsp butter	1 Tblsp sugar
2 cups milk	

Beat all the ingredients together and bake in a slow oven until brown. Serve with cream and sugar to taste.

Kaanga Roroi

1 Tblsp butter	1 small kumara, grated
Milk	1 cup minced cornmeal
1 Tblsp sugar	

Melt butter in milk and add sugar. Add kumara to cornmeal and mix with rest of ingredients to a nice consistency. Gather and clean corn leaves and drop 2 Tblsp of mixture into each of the leaves. Tie both ends then drop into boiling water and cook for 30 minutes. Kaanga roroi can be eaten hot or cold.

Kaanga Pungarehu

4 cups clean manuka wood ash

2 cups white corn

Add the corn to the ashes, add some water, and bring all to the boil in a saucepan. Reduce the heat and boil gently until the skin leaves the grain. Strain into clean cold water, rubbing the skins off the corn kernels. Return the corn to the saucepan and boil again in fresh water. Repeat this process three times, then boil gently until the grain swells to twice its size. Serve either hot or cold with cream and sugar.

Puha or Rauriki

The terms puha and rauriki are generally applied to both the smooth-leaved sow thistle and the prickly leaved sow thistle, which are also known as puha pororua and puha tiotio, respectively. Puha grows in the shade in long grass, or in damp, dark places, and is a common garden weed. The whole top of the young plant is cut off and has to be washed several times in clean water.

Puha Tiotio

Take a small basket of puha and wash it in 3–4 lots of water to make sure the puha is clean. Squeeze or rub the stalks to help remove any bitterness. Bring a pot of water to the boil. Add one handful of puha at a time and boil without the lid on the pot for 30–60 minutes. Strain the puha, cool, pack into plastic bags, seal and refrigerate.

For a quick luncheon, take some of the puha and chop finely, add precooked long-grain rice, salt and pepper to taste, and fry in oil. Delicious with any meat.

The water the puha is boiled in makes a lovely soup and is also a blood tonic.

Puha Penupenu

Boil some puha until soft; strain. Cook three potatoes, strain and mash with a little lard or butter. Combine puha with potatoes, mash together until smooth. This dish is good for babies aged 6 months to 2 years.

PUHA MARA

Wash some puha in plenty of water, and when clean put into a saucepan and boil for 5 minutes. Drain, refresh under cold running water, and return to the saucepan. Boil until all the bitterness is out. Drain and bottle with cut up mussels.

PUHA AND MUSSELS

Boil some puha in salted water for 1 hour. Drain. Lightly cook the shelled mussels and cut into pieces. Add the mussels to the puha with the water they were cooked in. Serve the next day with mashed potatoes.

PUHA TOROI

1 kg cooked puha

3 large mussels

Boil mussels in 600 ml water, remove from shells and cut or dice. Strip the puha leaves from the stalks, wash them thoroughly, and boil hard for about 5 seconds. Add mussels and let simmer for a very short time. Store in bottles without lids.

Using this method you can eat toroi almost immediately. However, if you leave it, you will find a white fungus will form on top. When you are ready to eat the toroi, simply remove the fungus.

Corned Beef, Puha and Kouka

1 piece corned beef *or* **brisket**

3 onions, chopped

1 Tblsp mustard

2 Tblsp vinegar

2 Tblsp sugar

Puha

Kouka

Potatoes

Boil a piece of corned beef or brisket and cut up into little pieces. Add onions, mustard, vinegar and sugar to the meat and when partially cooked add puha, kouka cut into halves, then potatoes. Continue boiling until all ingredients are cooked.

WATERCRESS

Found in fast flowing streams, watercress is a tasty relish and salad item.

WATERCRESS TOROI

Wash some watercress thoroughly, discarding stems and dry leaves. Cut into small pieces and put into a colander. Blanch with boiling water, put into a pot and cook for 10 minutes in salted water. Cut mussels into small pieces and mix into the watercress. This makes a delicious cold dish to have with bread and butter.

WATERCRESS SOUP

250 g peeled potatoes

500 ml milk

1 bunch watercress

Salt and pepper

30 g butter

Cut the potatoes into smallish pieces and boil in salted water until cooked. Drain and process potatoes in a blender (or press through a sieve). Pour in the milk and add the chopped watercress. Pour the soup back into the saucepan and bring to simmering point. Remove from heat, season, and stir in the butter before serving.

WATERCRESS SALAD

1 bunch watercress
3 Tblsp tarragon vinegar
1 Tblsp freshly ground salt and pepper
250g bacon, fried

Wash the watercress thoroughly, put into plastic bags, seal and refrigerate overnight. Combine the vinegar with seasonings. Place the watercress in a salad bowl, add the bacon and toss in salad dressing just before serving.

Birds

TITI, MUTTON BIRD OR SOOTY SHEARWATER

These birds range very widely over the ocean and are usually seen in large flocks, but the largest breeding grounds in New Zealand are found on Stewart Island, sometimes called the 'Mutton Bird Islands'. A great many of the blackish grey chicks are killed every year as their very fatty flesh is popular eating among Maori and pakeha alike. The flightless young chicks live in burrows in the ground and are easy prey for the commercial mutton birder. Only certain Maori tribes, to whom permission is given each year by the government, are permitted to kill these birds. They can, however, be readily bought in commercial fish-shops throughout the country.

TO COOK MUTTON BIRDS

FRESH BIRDS

Remove any feathers from the carcass. The mutton bird may be treated in the same way as wild duck, i.e. roasted with a savoury stuffing of breadcrumbs, or, for a change, apples and onions. Bake for 1 hour.

43

If you don't like the bird's salty taste, boil it briefly, simmer in fresh water until softish, and then grill the bird until brown and sizzling. Garnish with a white sauce made with white wine. Add into the sauce as many Stewart Island oysters as it can comfortably accommodate. Serve with deep fried potato chips and a tossed salad.

SALTED BIRDS

Place in cold water and bring to the boil. Cook for 1 hour. If very salty, change the water after 30 minutes.

Alternatively, boil the mutton bird in water, changing it three or four times, until the bird is tender (about 1 hour). Grill the bird briefly, if desired. Serve with puha, cabbage, kumara and potatoes cooked in the water used for boiling the birds.

MUTTON BIRD SUPREME

1 mutton bird

White sauce

2 Tblsp white wine

Boil the mutton bird for 30 minutes. Drain, and add clean water. Repeat the procedure until the bird is soft. Place under grill and brown. Stir the white wine into the white sauce, and pour over the bird. Serve with green salad and potato chips.

PUKEKO OR SWAMP HEN

PUKEKO STEW

Skin the bird. Cut off the legs, making sure that the sinews are removed (these are as sharp as fish bones). Cut the bird into joints, roll in flour and brown in hot fat along with several sliced onions. Drain off any surplus fat, cover the bird with water, season well and simmer until tender. Thicken the gravy with flour mixed to a paste with water.

Pork

POAKA TAHU (Preserved Pork)

Take a mixture of pork and beef dripping and render down in a large pot. When rendered, leave aside on a low heat. Cut some pork into chunks and boil in salted water until half cooked. Strain and, when cool, strip the rind off the meat. Put the pork chunks into the dripping and bring to the boil, making sure the pieces are moved around to prevent sticking. Remove from the heat and leave to cool. Pour pork and dripping into clean containers and seal. The longer this meat is left the better. Delicious when heated up with puha or any greens.

Tao Mana

1 leg pork, flap on
4 slices white bread, 1 cm thick
170 ml white wine
8 dried apricots
1 small onion
1 small stick celery
Salt and pepper
1 tsp salt, extra
1 Tblsp oil

Remove the upper leg bone to form a pocket in the pork, but leave part of the flap on. Remove the crust from the bread, cut into 1 cm cubes, place in a shallow dish and cover with the wine. Allow to soak for 5–10 minutes, then drain off the surplus wine and reserve. Chop the apricots, onions and celery finely, and mix with the bread and seasoning. Stuff the cavity in the leg of pork with this, pulling the flap over; secure by sewing with coarse thread or with skewers. Score the pork rind and rub with the extra salt and oil. Have the oven pre-heated to 200°C, put the roast in, and reduce the oven setting to 180°C. Bake for 4–5 hours.

Serve with a gravy made from the pan brownings, water and the reserved wine. Thicken with cornflour. Accompany with stuffed apricots: combine half a carton of sour cream with 1 Tblsp of peanut butter; use this to fill the centres of 8–10 dried apricots.

Shellfish

A Word of Caution

Mussels, oysters and paua have a high percentage of protein, but shellfish easily harbour bacteria. For this reason, it is important they be collected in areas where there is no danger of contamination from such things as sewerage outlets. Cases of typhoid have been traced to indiscriminate collecting and use of shellfish from doubtful areas. If you are not certain of the status of shellfish areas near you, play safe and buy them from the supermarket or fishmonger. Whether you buy or collect shellfish, be sure to keep them cool, and use them as soon as possible.

Collection limits

The government has set restrictions on the numbers of shellfish that can be collected. By adhering to these limits we can ensure that shellfish are available for future generations of New Zealanders to enjoy. Complete regulations are available from Bennetts Bookshop Ltd (formerly the Government Bookshop), but a pamphlet covering the essential aspects of the restrictions can be obtained free of charge from the Ministry of Fisheries.

The following table summarises the maximum number of shellfish you can collect in any one day:

Shellfish species	Maximum limit per person per day	Other restrictions
COCKLES	150	
KINA	50	
MUSSELS	50	Cannot be collected using underwater breathing apparatus except snorkel.
OYSTERS (dredge)	50	Must be greater than 58 mm in diameter; must be landed in the shell; in the South Island can only be taken between 1 March and 31 August.
OYSTERS (rock and pacific)	250	Must be removed from the rock before opening; can be collected all year round except in the Hauraki Gulf, Whangaruru Harbour and the Bay of Islands, where there are restrictions.
PAUA	10	Must be greater than 125 mm in diameter; must be landed in the shell; cannot be collected using underwater breathing apparatus except snorkel.
PIPI	150	
SCALLOPS	20	Must be greater than 100 mm in diameter; must be landed in the shell; can only be collected between 15 July and 14 February.
TOHEROA	0	There is currently a total ban on the collection of toheroa.
TUATUA	150	

KINA (TORETORE)

The kina or sea egg is found on rocks and under ledges at low tide. At certain times of the year there is a larger edible portion than at others. The early spring is a particularly good time to gather this shellfish, which is covered with spikes. Open it with a sharp knife, and when you shake it you will see the edible part clinging to the sides. The colour of this material varies from yellow, through pinkish brown to dark brown. It can be easily scooped out with a spoon. When cooking, care should be taken to keep kina apart from other victuals.

BAKED KINA

Fill a pie dish with alternate layers of kina and bread-crumbs, with the last layer being breadcrumbs. Put generous knobs of butter all over the top, place in a hot oven, then reduce the heat and bake for 30–45 minutes or until set. Be careful not to overcook this dish, otherwise the kina become indigestible.

KINA SOUP

12 kina	600 ml milk
Salt and pepper	1 pkt Maggi Pea and Ham Soup
1 cup cream	

Remove the large kina 'tongues', mash, and season with salt and pepper. Mix cream and milk together in a pot and heat. Do not allow to boil. Mix soup with a little of the cream and milk, add this to the rest of the cream and milk. Add the mashed kina.

Kuku (Mussels)

There are a number of mussels found in New Zealand's rocky coasts, estuaries and harbours, but the best known commercially are the horse mussel, which lies buried in colonies near the low water mark in sheltered areas, and the blue mussel, which is found on most rocky shores, but forms extensive beds only in the southern part of the country. In more exposed habitats it is replaced by the green mussel, e.g. in western parts of the South Island. Only in a few localities are mussels exposed at low tide.

Preserved Mussels

Place the mussels in a saucepan without water. Put on a hot element and cover with a cloth. When the mussels start to open, drain the juice into a container and immediately run cold water over the mussels. Shell and place into preserving jars. Cover with two parts mussel juice and one part vinegar. Leave the jars unsealed and keep in the refrigerator.

Mussel Soup

1 onion, chopped	Parsley
1 knob butter	1 tsp ground ginger
2 mussels, chopped	Milk

Place the onion into a little water, add butter, mussels, parsley, ground ginger and sufficient milk. Don't boil. Thicken with a little cornflour. Serve with toast.

COLD WEATHER KUKU

2 large onions, finely chopped
1 Tblsp butter
1 litre milk
$^1/_2$ tsp salt
$^1/_4$ tsp pepper
1 tsp curry powder
Cornflour
18 mussels

Light fry onions in butter, add milk, salt, pepper and curry powder. Bring to the boil; add cornflour to thicken to desired consistency. When cooked add fresh, raw, shelled and coarsely chopped mussels. Serve immediately.

MUSSEL DIP

12 cooked mussels
$^1/_2$ cup white wine
1 tsp salt
4 peppercorns
2 cloves
1 sprig thyme
1 bay leaf
1 sprig parsley
1 onion, sliced
1 carrot, sliced

1 clove garlic, crushed

2 Tblsp tomato sauce

1 Tblsp Worcestershire sauce

Chilli pepper

Trim the mussels and put them in the fridge to chill. In a pot, combine $\frac{3}{4}$ cup water with the wine, salt, peppercorns, cloves, thyme, bay leaf, parsley, onion, and carrot. Boil 30 minutes, add garlic and tomato sauce; boil until reduced to $\frac{3}{4}$ cup. Add Worcestershire sauce and chilli pepper to taste. Chill. Serve the sauce cold in a small bowl in the centre of a plate and surround with the mussels. Dip mussels in sauce to eat.

MUSSELS IN BATTER

12 mussels

1 egg

2 Tblsp flour

2 Tblsp milk

Salt and pepper

1 tsp cream of tartar

Oil for deep frying

Clean mussels and remove beards. Beat the egg and add flour, milk, seasoning and cream of tartar. Dip mussels in batter and fry in hot fat.

FRIED MUSSELS (VERSION 1)

6 large mussels	¼ cup milk
Flour	1 cup crushed breakfast cereal
1 egg, beaten	30 g butter

Place the mussels in a saucepan with a ½ cup of water and heat until the mussels open. Strain the liquid from the mussels. Take the mussels from their shells and remove the outer ring around the edge. Flour the mussels and dip into combined egg and milk. Coat with crushed cereal crumbs and fry in hot melted butter until light golden brown.

FRIED MUSSELS (VERSION 2)

18 mussels	2 eggs, beaten
1 cup flour	Breadcrumbs
Salt and pepper	60 g dripping

Shell the mussels and remove the beards; blanch for 2 minutes in boiling water and strain. Run through cold water and drain. Try to keep the mussels in tidy pieces. Dust the mussels with flour and add salt and pepper. Dip the mussels in the eggs then coat with breadcrumbs. Put dripping into the pan and, when smoking hot, add the mussels. Fry until golden brown and serve with hot chips, tomatoes and lemon wedges.

Deep-Fried Mussels Béarnaise

48 large mussels

2 Tblsp shallots, chopped

2 sprigs thyme

2 sprigs parsley

1 bay leaf

Salt

150 ml dry white wine

250 g green bacon

Freshly ground black pepper

Flour

1 egg, beaten

Breadcrumbs

Béarnaise sauce

Scrape, beard and wash mussels and place in a saucepan with shallots, thyme, parsley and bay leaf. Season lightly with salt and moisten with dry white wine. Cover saucepan and steam 4–5 minutes, or until shells have opened.

Remove mussels from their shells; dice green bacon; thread small skewers with alternate mussels and bacon pieces. Season to taste with freshly ground black pepper. Roll in flour; dip in beaten egg and then in dry breadcrumbs. Thread skewers on a piece of string and fry in deep fat until golden. Serve with béarnaise sauce.

SCALLOPED MUSSELS

24 mussels	2 cups milk
2 Tblsp butter	Breadcrumbs
2 heaped Tblsp flour	
Salt, pepper and cayenne	
pepper to taste	

Put mussels in a saucepan without water and heat until the shells open. Cool, remove the mussels from the shells, remove the beards and put the mussels in a pie dish. In a separate saucepan melt the butter, add flour, salt, pepper and cayenne. Add milk gradually, stirring until smooth. Cook until thick, stirring all the time. Pour the sauce over the mussels, cover with breadcrumbs and a few small pieces of butter. Bake until light brown in a hot oven for 10–15 minutes. Serve hot.

MUSSEL PIE

4 or 5 mussels	Salt and pepper
2 eggs, beaten	Parsley, chopped
1 cup milk	Pastry

Prepare the mussels, removing all tough parts, and chop into pieces. Beat the eggs with the milk and seasonings and mix together with the parsley and mussels. Pour into a pastry-lined pie dish and cover with pastry. Bake 20 minutes in a moderate oven.

KAKAHI (FRESHWATER MUSSELS)

Kakahi is a black fresh water mussel. Paua or pipi can be used as a substitute.

KAKAHI SOUP

2 cups kakahi

2 large onions

1 cup grated carrot

2 Tblsp brown sugar

2 Tblsp Worcestershire sauce

2 Tblsp vinegar

Dash of cayenne pepper

Salt and pepper to taste

Cornflour

Boil kakahi until well cooked, then strain, retaining the juice for the soup. Fry onions in peanut oil until light and transparent. Add the onions and all remaining ingredients to the mussel juice, and bring to the boil. Thicken to desired consistency with cornflour, add chopped parsley and serve.

OYSTERS

OYSTER SOUP

12 oysters	6 cups fish stock
Juice of 1 lemon	1 Tblsp butter
Small glass dry white wine	2 Tblsp flour
Salt and pepper	

Add lemon juice to oysters and set aside. Add wine, salt and pepper to stock. Bring to boil then quickly reduce heat and simmer 5 minutes. In a separate saucepan melt butter; add flour. Slowly stir in stock and bring just to boiling point. Just before serving add oysters.

OYSTER SAUCE

3 Tblsp butter	1 tsp salt
$\frac{1}{2}$ tsp celery salt	3 Tblsp flour
$\frac{1}{2}$ tsp paprika	300 ml milk
$\frac{1}{4}$ tsp cayenne	18 oysters
Pepper	Lemon juice

Melt butter with seasonings. Blend in flour. Gradually stir in milk. Cook, stirring constantly until thick and smooth. Add drained oysters and a little oyster juice if required. Add lemon juice to taste; check seasoning before serving. Makes about 2 cups.

OYSTERS ROCKEFELLER

4 Tblsp finely chopped shallots

120 g butter

4 Tblsp breadcrumbs

4 Tblsp chopped celery leaves

4 Tblsp chopped parsley

1 bunch watercress

1 tsp finely chopped chervil

1 tsp finely chopped tarragon

4 Tblsp Pernod

Salt, freshly ground black pepper and cayenne pepper

24 fresh oysters

Rock salt

Sauté shallots in 4 Tblsp of the butter until transparent, add breadcrumbs and stir over a low heat until lightly browned. Finely chop celery, parsley and watercress leaves, separated from their stems. Combine shallot and breadcrumb mixture with chopped greens in a large bowl or mortar, add finely chopped chervil and tarragon, Pernod, and salt, pepper and cayenne pepper to taste. Add remaining butter and pound to a smooth paste. Keep cool until ready to use.

Place a bed of rock salt in a baking tin large enough to hold the oysters comfortably, or in four small tins. Dampen salt slightly and place oysters, opened, on this bed. Place 1 Tblsp of the green herb butter on each oyster and bake in at 220°C for 4–5 minutes, or until butter has melted and oysters are heated through. Serve immediately.

Oyster Stew

450 ml oyster liquor

1.2 litre oysters

450 ml milk

4 Tblsp butter

150 ml cream

Salt and freshly ground black pepper

Cayenne pepper

Strain oyster liquor into a large saucepan. Wash oysters thoroughly and add to liquor. Simmer over low heat for 5 minutes. Add milk, and heat thoroughly, but do not allow to boil. Stir in butter and cream; add salt and pepper to taste and a dash of cayenne pepper.

Paua

The paua is a univalve shellfish with a large oval flattened shell up to 14 cm long, its inner surface bright with opalescent greens, blues and pinks. The outer surface of the shellfish itself is sooty black, but inside the flesh is quite white, but very tough. It is very good eating if properly prepared and cooked. It can be obtained only at low water or spring tides, otherwise it has to be dived for. Remove the paua from its hold on the rock by sliding a broad bladed knife underneath and levering off quickly. Use a sharp knife to remove the fish (pewa or sac) from the shell and pull off the paua. Scrape and clean. Pulverise paua between clean cloths with a heavy wooden mallet until soft.

To Freeze Paua

Cook the paua in boiling water for a few minutes to free from shells. Cool and mince. Pack in plastic bags in sufficient quantities for making fritters. Remove any air and fasten tight.

Self-Pressure Cooked Paua

Shell the required amount of paua, remove the waste from the base of the paua, wash and replace in shells. Melt a little butter in a pan, place the paua face down, using the shells as covers. Cook for 15–20 minutes or longer depending on the size of the paua. Remove from shells and serve immediately.

Barbecued Paua with Onions

Shell the paua and tenderise. Melt a little butter or dripping on the barbecue hot plate and cook the paua slowly. When the paua is just about cooked, put onion rings on the hotplate and cook together until the paua is tender. Serve hot with potato chips, fried bread, salt and pepper to taste.

Creme Paua

Prepare sufficient paua for the number of people to be served. Put some butter into a frying pan and lightly fry paua with some finely chopped onions, then season to taste. Remove from the pan, add milk and thicken with cornflour mixed with milk; cook. Return the paua to the frying pan. Serve on toast or as an entree.

Fried Paua

Fry paua in very hot fat, being careful to keep a lid over the pan, as they splutter a lot. When cooked on one side, turn and reduce the heat. Serve hot.

PAUA STEAKS (VERSION 1)

Using a rolling pin or hammer, beat the white part of three paua to a pulp. Slice into long thin strips. Roll in salted flour and fry in hot butter, allowing 5 seconds each side. Serve with mashed potatoes, kumara, pumpkin and green or butter beans. Garnish with sliced tomatoes.

PAUA STEAKS (VERSION 2)

Pound 6 paua until soft. Put 2 Tblsp oil into a frying pan. Fry paua lightly, turn until both sides are cooked. Do not have oil too hot or the paua will harden. Delicious with pineapple rings or fried bananas.

PAUA SOUP (version 1)

1 celery stick, chopped	1 potato
2 small onions	500 ml milk
Butter	Salt and pepper
1 carrot	Minced paua

Boil the celery until tender. Fry the onions in butter until golden brown. Grate the carrot and potato. Heat the milk and when a skin forms add all ingredients except for the paua. Bring to the boil, then add the paua. Simmer for 5 minutes. Serve with potato crisps or toast fingers.

PAUA SOUP (version 2)

12–18 paua	120 g butter, melted
1 large onion, chopped	1/2 cup flour
Herbs	450 ml milk
Salt and pepper	

Place the paua and onion in a muslin bag, and put this into 2 litres of water; add the herbs, salt and pepper to taste and simmer for 30 minutes. In a separate pot, melt the butter, stir in the flour and cook for 1 minute; gradually add the milk and bring to the boil, stirring constantly until the sauce thickens. Remove the muslin bag and pour the sauce into the pan of stock. Simmer gently for 5–10 minutes. Add more seasoning if required, including a pinch of cayenne and mace if desired.

Paua Fritters (VERSION 1)

  3 paua
  2 medium-sized onions
  1 egg, beaten
  2 or 3 cloves garlic, crushed
  Salt and pepper
  Flour

Pound the paua, cut into quarters and put through mincer. Place in a bowl with finely chopped onions, egg, garlic, salt and pepper. Mix in a little flour to thicken. Heat oil in a pan. Drop in tablespoonfuls of the mixture. Cook gently for about 3 minutes on each side. Serve.

Paua Fritters (VERSION 2)

  2 eggs
  ½ cup milk
  2 cups flour
  2 tsp baking powder
  Salt and pepper
  4 paua

Beat eggs well and add milk, flour, baking powder and seasonings, mixing until smooth in texture. Put four paua in a pot of boiling water for 2–4 minutes to free them from their shells. When cool, mince and add to batter. Fry spoonfuls of the mixture in hot fat until cooked.

Paua Fritters (version 3)

8 paua
1 onion
1 cup flour
1 tsp baking powder
1 tsp salt
1 egg
Milk

Mince the paua and onion. Make a batter with flour, baking powder, salt, egg and milk. Add paua and onion. Put tablespoons of the mixture into a pan with hot fat and cook until brown on both sides. Serve.

Paua Fritters (version 4)

1 egg
½ cup milk
Salt and pepper
Flour
½ tsp baking powder
6 paua, minced

Make a batter with egg, milk, salt and pepper; add flour to make a consistency similar to cream; lastly add baking powder. Add the paua, and fry in very hot fat for about 5 minutes. Drain and serve hot.

Paua Pancakes

2 cups flour	½ tsp salt
4 eggs	Milk
3 Tblsp baking powder	6 paua, minced

Put flour into a mixing bowl and make a well in the centre. Add eggs, baking powder, and salt; beat well, adding sufficient milk to make a pancake mixture. Put a pan on the stove and grease. Pour a ladleful of mixture into the pan, take a spoonful of paua and pour into the centre of the pancake. Quickly add another spoonful of pancake mixture over the top and fry until cooked.

Savoury Dip and Minced Paua

Paua	Salt and pepper
Stale bread	1 tin Nestlé Reduced Cream
Flour	1 pkt Maggi Onion Soup

Place paua in a pot of cold water, bring to the boil, cook until they lift out of their shells easily, clean and put through a mincer with some slices of stale bread. Mix with salt and pepper and enough flour to allow the mixture to be moulded into little patties. Fry in oil until brown on both sides. Alternatively, the minced paua may be cooked in a pancake batter without sugar. Make the dip by combining cream and soup mix thoroughly.

PICKLED PAUA

2 cups minced *or* finely chopped paua

1½ cups vinegar

½ cup golden syrup

½ cup flour

½ Tblsp curry powder

2 Tblsp mustard

Boil the paua in the vinegar for 15–20 minutes. Add the rest of the ingredients and mix together. Boil for a further 10 minutes, bottle and seal.

CREAMED PAUA

2 Tblsp butter

2 Tblsp flour

1 cup milk

Salt and pepper

1 large onion, sliced thinly

500 g paua, minced

½ cup cream

Melt the butter in a pan, add the flour and cook for 1 minute. Slowly add the milk, salt, pepper, and the onion. Bring to the boil, stirring constantly until the sauce thickens. Add the paua and stir thoroughly. Add the cream, bring to boiling point and stand aside, covered, until the paua is cooked. Serve with rice or mashed potatoes and parsley.

CREAMED PAUA AND BACON

6 rashers bacon
12 paua, cleaned and tenderised
300 ml cream

Place the bacon in a frypan, flour the paua and place on top. Cook gently for 5–10 minutes or until tender. Pour the cream over and simmer for 5 minutes. Serve.

PAUA IN CREAM

1 kg paua
30 g butter
1 onion
600 ml cream
2 Tblsp cornflour
¾ cup milk
Salt and pepper

Slice the prepared paua into small pieces. Melt the butter in a saucepan and add finely chopped onion. Fry until golden brown. Add chopped paua and toss quickly to sauté evenly. Add cream, and heat to just below boiling point. Thicken with cornflour mixed to a paste with milk. Add seasoning and serve immediately. Do not overcook as this toughens the paua.

Paua with Pineapple Sauce

12 paua	1 Tblsp flour, extra
Flour	1 can of pineapple rings
60 g butter	Salt and pepper

Take the clean paua and place on a breadboard. With two dinner forks, one held in each hand, fork the paua well on both sides. Toss paua generously with flour and fry in butter for 15 minutes turning over halfway through. Arrange paua on a meat dish or casserole lid and leave in a warm oven.

Make the sauce: remove any excess fat from the pan. Add the extra flour, $\frac{1}{2}$ cup pineapple juice, salt and pepper, and mix to a paste. Add 1 Tblsp warm water, stir, then return to cook over a low heat, stirring constantly to prevent lumps. When thickened, pour the sauce over the paua and use the pineapple rings to garnish. Serve hot. Also delicious with baked kumara.

Paua Casserole

1 kg paua	1 medium onion, finely chopped
$\frac{1}{4}$ cup flour	300 ml fish stock
Salt and pepper	

Chop the paua into quarters, and place in a paper bag with flour and seasonings. Coat well. Fry the paua pieces in oil for about 5 minutes, remove and place in a fireproof casserole dish. Fry the onions and add to the paua. Shake the flour and seasonings from the bag and stir them into the remaining sediment in the pan.

Slowly add fish stock to make a light sauce; stir until sauce thickens. Pour sauce over the paua. Cover and cook slowly for 1½ hours at 120–150°C. This long cooking time helps to tenderise the paua. If the sauce needs thickening at the end of cooking, add cornflour blended in a little milk. Cream (about 2 Tblsp) may also be added at the end. Serve this as an entree on plain boiled rice.

Paua and Meat Pie

1 clove garlic	Crushed pineapple
250 g mutton, diced	Grated cheese
4 paua, minced	2 potatoes, thinly sliced
2 onions, finely chopped	Pastry
2 carrots, grated	

Rub a pie dish all over with garlic and cover the bottom with the mutton pieces, then with minced paua, onions and carrots. Finally add pineapple pieces, cheese and ½ cup water. Slice the potatoes on top and then cover with pie crust. Bake in a preheated oven for 20 minutes. Serve.

PIPI

The pipi was one of the favourite foods of the early Maori settlers, judging from their presence in the middens, or 'rubbish dumps'. The pipi can be readily identified by its shape: oblong with rounded ends and an apex in the middle, rather than towards one end as with the tuangi, hehari and other similar species. Like the tuangi, the pipi is found in sandy or muddy beds between low and half tides by feeling for them with your feet and picking them up quickly by hand.

PIPI APPETISERS

Place pipi in a large pot and clamp on lid. Allow the pipi to steam. Remove the shellfish and place in a container. Place in the warmer of an electric stove to enable fish to dehydrate gradually. Sun drying is preferable if time is plentiful. If properly prepared, the pipi are very tasty and rattle like beads when poured into a dish. They are very tasty when served with sprigs of watercress.

PIPI AND CURRY STEW

Shell pipi into a pot; collect the juice in the same pot. Finely slice one onion and add to the pipi. If more juice is needed, add water; boil until cooked. Thicken with a paste made from water, flour and curry powder. Serve hot with cooked rice and vegetables.

PIPI SOUP (VERSION 1)

Gather the pipi and place in cold water to rid the shellfish of sand. Steam in a pot, and when the pipi are open allow the sand to settle, then remove the meat from the shells. Strain the juice in to a pot and simmer gently. Add milk, mixed vegetables and seasoning, and thicken with cornflour.

PIPI SOUP (VERSION 2)

1 cup freshly shelled pipi

1 onion, chopped

1 sprig parsley

1 cup milk

2 Tblsp cornflour

30g butter

½ tsp nutmeg

Salt and pepper

Mince the pipi, place in a saucepan with 2 cups of water, onion and parsley and simmer gently for 30 minutes. When cooked, press through a sieve or puree in a blender and return to pan. Blend 2 Tblsp milk with cornflour and add to pipi puree with remaining milk, butter, and nutmeg. Bring to boil, stirring continuously. Add salt and pepper to taste. Serve hot.

PIPI LUNCHEON DISH

Pipi
1 onion
2 carrots
1 cauliflower
1 cabbage
Salt and pepper
2 Tblsp cornflour

Shell enough pipi for the number of people you are serving; retain the juice. Finely chop the onion and carrots; cut the cauliflower into florets, and shred the cabbage. Fry the vegetables in a small amount of oil or butter. Add the pipi juice, season to taste. Blend the cornflour with a small amount of water, add to the juice and heat until thickened, stirring constantly. Drop in the pipi and heat through briefly before serving.

PUPU (CAT'S EYE)

The familiar cat's eye is named for its shell sealing plate. Pupu become less numerous, but larger, in southern parts of the country.

PRESERVED COCKLES

Pupu	1 Tblsp sugar
1 cup vinegar	

Gather good sized pupu (or any other cockles), clean and put into a saucepan of cold water. Bring to boil for a few seconds and then turn the heat off but leave the lid on the pot to allow the shellfish to steam. When cold shell the cockles. Combine vinegar, 1 cup of water and sugar. Bring to the boil, add prepared cockles and boil for 2 minutes then bottle. Delicious with bread and butter.

COCKLE FRITTERS

4 Tblsp self-raising flour	Milk
½ tsp salt	1 egg
½ tsp pepper	1 cup shelled raw cockles

Mix flour, salt and pepper with enough milk to make a batter consistency. Add egg and mix well. Mix in raw cockles. Deep fry in hot fat.

Scallops

The commercially exploited scallops are bivalves which usually live in beds near the high tide mark of harbours and estuaries. There are several types of scallops and most are edible, the best part being the muscle which closes the valves.

Poached Scallops

> 500 g scallops, shelled and cleaned
> 450 ml milk
> Salt and pepper to taste
> ½ tsp curry powder, optional
> 1 Tblsp flour
> 1 Tblsp cornflour

Cut scallops into small pieces, put into a pot with the milk and bring slowly to the boil. Add salt, pepper and curry, stirring all the time. Make a paste with flour and cornflour and a small amount of milk or water, and add to the scallops once they have boiled for 3 minutes or are cooked. Stir constantly. If desired, pour the scallops into a casserole dish, sprinkle with grated cheese and paprika, and grill until cheese bubbles. Serve hot.

VARIATIONS
Replace the curry powder with parsley, or 60–90 g grated tasty cheese, or 30 g grated cheese and 3 Tblsp cream sherry.

BASIC POACHED SCALLOPS

8–10 scallops	1 bouquet garni
300 ml dry white wine	Salt and freshly ground
½ onion, chopped	black pepper

Wash and trim scallops. Drain. Place in a saucepan with dry white wine and enough water barely to cover scallops. Add chopped onion and bouquet garni and season to taste with salt and freshly ground black pepper. Bring slowly to the boil and simmer gently for 5 minutes or until tender. Drain the scallops, straining and reserving the liquor. Slice scallops if they are large and use as directed in any of the following recipes.

BAKED SCALLOPS

Basic poached scallops
2 Tblsp butter
2 Tblsp olive oil
1 clove garlic, finely chopped
2 Tblsp finely chopped parsley
2 Tblsp fresh breadcrumbs
Salt and freshly ground black pepper

Prepare scallops as directed. Heat butter and olive oil in a heat-proof baking dish until butter sizzles. Slice scallops thickly and toss in dish with garlic, parsley and breadcrumbs. Season to taste with salt and freshly ground black pepper, and bake under the grill until scallops are golden.

CURRIED SCALLOPS

Basic poached scallops
2 Tblsp butter
2 Tblsp flour
$\frac{1}{4}$–$\frac{1}{2}$ level tsp curry powder
4–6 Tblsp double cream
Salt and freshly ground black pepper
Parsley, finely chopped

Prepare scallops as directed. Melt butter in the top of a double saucepan; stir in flour and curry powder, and cook over simmering water, stirring continuously, until roux is well blended.

Add enough scallop liquor (about 300 ml) to make a smooth, rich sauce. Add cream, sliced scallops, and salt and freshly ground black pepper to taste. Fill scallop shells or individual ramekins with this mixture and sprinkle with parsley.

SCALLOP SALAD

 Basic poached scallops
 3 Tblsp olive oil
 1 Tblsp wine vinegar
 Salt and freshly ground black pepper
 Mayonnaise
 Lettuce leaves

Prepare scallops as directed. Drain, slice and while still warm, toss in a bowl with olive oil, vinegar, salt and pepper, to taste. Chill. Just before serving, add mayonnaise and toss. Serve in a lettuce-lined bowl.

SCALLOPS IN JACKETS

 5 large scallops
 Prosciutto ham, thinly sliced
 Butter
 Buttered toast
 Parsley, chopped

Wrap each scallop in prosciutto and secure with a toothpick. Sauté lightly in butter until scallops are tender, about 20 minutes. Serve hot on buttered toast sprinkled with parsley.

GRILLED SCALLOPS

8 scallops
Butter
Salt and freshly ground black pepper
4 slices hot buttered toast
1 Tblsp parsley, finely chopped
Lemon juice

Wash and trim scallops; dry carefully. Place on a buttered baking tin. Dot with butter, season to taste with salt and freshly ground black pepper. Pre-heat grill; place scallops about 8 cm from heat and grill for 4–6 minutes, or until scallops become lightly browned. To serve place on hot buttered toast and sprinkle with parsley and lemon juice.

SCALLOP KEBABS

16 scallops
120 g butter, melted
4 Tblsp dried breadcrumbs
Parsley, finely chopped
¼ tsp dried marjoram
Grated rind of ½ lemon
Salt and freshly ground black pepper
4–8 rashers green bacon
Melted butter
Lemon juice

Dip washed and dried scallops in melted butter and then in dry breadcrumbs mixed with parsley, marjoram and lemon rind. Season to taste with salt and freshly ground black pepper. Arrange four scallops on each skewer with one or two rashers of green bacon, weaving the bacon slice back and forth between the scallops. Grill scallops lightly over charcoal or under the grill, basting with melted butter and turning the skewers frequently while cooking. Serve with melted butter seasoned with lemon juice and parsley.

FRIED SCALLOPS

8 scallops
2 eggs, beaten
4 Tblsp cream
Salt and freshly ground black pepper
Cornmeal, biscuit crumbs *or* fresh breadcrumbs
120 g butter
150 ml oil

Wash and trim scallops; slice in half. Combine beaten eggs and cream in a bowl. Add salt and freshly ground black pepper to taste. Dip scallops in egg mixture, then in cornmeal or crumbs, and allow to set on aluminium foil for about 5 minutes before cooking. Melt butter in a thick-bottomed frying pan or deep-fryer. Add oil; bring to frying temperature and cook scallops in fat until golden brown. Serve immediately with wedges of lemon.

Scallops Mornay

2 Tblsp butter

2 Tblsp flour

$\frac{1}{2}$ tsp mustard

Dash cayenne pepper

1 cup milk

$\frac{1}{2}$ tsp salt

$\frac{1}{2}$ tsp Worcestershire sauce

$\frac{1}{2}$ cup grated cheese

1 small onion, finely chopped

1 tsp butter, extra

$\frac{1}{2}$ cup white wine *or* lemon juice and enough water
  to make $\frac{1}{2}$ cup liquid

500g scallops, fresh if possible

1 tsp chopped parsley

$\frac{1}{4}$ tsp salt, extra

$\frac{1}{4}$ tsp pepper

$\frac{3}{4}$ cup grated mild cheese or parmesan cheese, extra

First, make the mornay sauce. Melt the butter in a saucepan, then add the flour and cook for 1 minute, stirring constantly. Blend in the mustard powder and cayenne pepper, then slowly add the milk, stirring constantly. Bring to the boil and simmer until the sauce thickens, all the while stirring. Remove from the heat, add the salt, Worcestershire sauce and the cheese. Stir to combine then set aside.

Sauté onion in extra butter until tender, Add wine or lemon

juice and water. Add scallops and cook gently for 5 minutes. (If scallops are large, cut into 2 or 3 pieces.) Remove scallops and continue cooking liquid until it is reduced to approximately 3 Tblsp. Add mornay sauce, scallops parsley, extra salt and pepper, and mix well. Place this mixture into six scallop shells or small ramekin dishes and sprinkle extra cheese on top. Grill until top begins to bubble.

SCALLOPS AND MUSHROOMS IN WHITE WINE

500 g scallops

450 ml milk

12 button mushrooms, thinly sliced

2 Tblsp finely chopped parsley

4 shallots, finely chopped

4 Tblsp butter

2 Tblsp flour

4 Tblsp cream

Fresh breadcrumbs

Butter, extra

Poach the scallops in the milk for 3 minutes or until cooked. Drain the scallops, reserving the stock. Sauté sliced mushrooms, parsley and finely chopped shallots in butter until golden. Blend in flour and add the reserved stock very slowly, stirring constantly. Stir in cream. Combine scallops with the sauce in a baking dish, sprinkle with breadcrumbs, dot with extra butter and brown under the grill.

Toheroa

The toheroa is the largest bivalve to be found on the driftline of some of the sandy beaches of the North Island's west coast. Its ability to burrow rapidly enables it to exploit this very unstable environment.

The tuatua and pipi are smaller members of the same family, and they can be substituted for toheroa in all of these recipes.

The collection of toheroa is currently forbidden. Contact the Department of Fisheries to find out whether or not a season will be declared.

To Prepare Toheroa

Toheroa need to be washed thoroughly after shelling. First immerse them in clear water, then cover with boiling water and allow to stand for 2 minutes. Drain off the water and cover immediately with a second lot of boiling water. As soon as the first shells snap open, pour the water off and retain it. Open all the shells, remove the toheroa 'muscles' and return them to the reserved water until required.

Steamed Toheroa

Wash the toheroa well and place in a large saucepan. Cover with hot water and leave for 2 minutes. Pour off the water and cover with boiling water. Put the lid on and wrap saucepan in a towel. Leave for three hours.

TOHEROA SOUP (VERSION 1)

25 g butter	Pinch of curry powder
1 Tblsp flour	Pinch of cayenne pepper
1 cup milk	1 cup tinned toheroa pulp
Salt and pepper	or 1–2 cups fresh toheroa
Pinch of nutmeg	Cream for garnish

Heat the butter in a saucepan, stir in the flour and cook until the mixture bubbles. Gradually stir in the milk and cook until the sauce thickens. Season with salt and pepper, add nutmeg, curry, cayenne and blend in the toheroa. Reheat, but do not boil. Serve hot, garnished with a swirl of cream.

TOHEROA SOUP (VERSION 2)

12 toheroa	1.2 litre fish stock
60 g butter	Salt and pepper
60 g flour	Pinch of thyme

Mince the toheroa. Melt the butter, blend in the flour and cook for 1 minute. Gradually add the stock, stirring constantly. Add seasonings and toheroa and cook gently for 5–10 minutes. Strain, reheat and serve.

TOHEROA CHOWDER

2 large onions	12 toheroa, minced
2 ripe tomatoes	1 tsp ground mace
1 Tblsp butter or dripping	Pepper and salt to taste

Chop onions finely; stand tomatoes in hot water for a few minutes, then slip off the skins; cut into rounds. Fry the onions until golden brown in butter or dripping, then fry the tomatoes for 10 minutes. Add minced toheroa, mace, pepper and salt. Fry for a further 10 minutes, stirring occasionally. Serve very hot on buttered toast or fried bread.

TOHEROA FRITTERS

12 toheroa, minced

1 onion, finely chopped

2 eggs, beaten

$\frac{1}{2}$ cup milk or beer

1 cup flour

1 tsp baking powder

Salt and pepper

Mix all the ingredients together. Fry spoonfuls in hot fat or butter. Quickly brown both sides. Drain on brown paper and serve with lemon wedges or tomato sauce.

TOHEROA PATTIES

    20 toheroa
    3–4 rashers of bacon
    2 large onions
    Parsley, optional
    3–4 eggs, beaten
    Salt and pepper
    $^{3}/_{4}$ cup flour
    $^{1}/_{2}$ tsp baking powder
    Milk

Mince the toheroa, bacon, onion and parsley. Add eggs and seasoning, flour, baking powder and enough milk to make a thick batter, then fry.

Mussels may be used instead of toheroa.

Tuangi

The tuangi is a round and plump shellfish which is often confused with the pipi. Tuangi are light grey on the outside; inside the shell there is a pronounced blue-purple mottling. The tuangi is found barely buried in sand or mud all along the coast of New Zealand, particularly in sandy bays and harbours, between low and half tide. They are a very clean type of food, but reasonable care has to be taken as to where they are collected because of the dangers from pollution. Keep only the bigger ones.

To Clean Tuangi

To remove sand and grit from the shellfish stand them in fresh water for a few hours or even overnight.

Steamed Tuangi

Gather good sized tuangi, clean them, arrange in a single layer in the bottom of a pan or saucepan and cover with cold water. Heat; in a few minutes they will have steamed open in their own juices and be ready to eat. While you are eating the first lot, a second serving can go into the pan. Eat with fresh bread and butter, and a dip of vinegar, seasoned with salt and pepper to taste.

Golden Tuangi Batter Balls

½ cup flour

½ cup cornflour

2 Tblsp baking powder

1 egg, beaten

1 Tblsp salad *or* cooking oil

Sift flour, cornflour and baking powder into a bowl. Make a well in the centre and stir in the egg, ⅓–½ cup of water and then the oil. Let the batter stand for 20 minutes. Open the shellfish (72 will make 12 fritters). Place in a sieve over a bowl to drain off as much of the liquid as possible. Mince the shellfish and add to the batter mix. If this mix becomes too thick after standing, thin it with the liquid drained from the tuangi. Drop spoonfuls into deep hot fat or oil, and serve with a summer salad.

Koura
(Crayfish)

The Maori term koura refers to both freshwater crayfish and saltwater crayfish. Freshwater crayfish can be found in many different habitats — swamps, rivers, lakes and streams — and are usually gathered from where they have hidden under stones in the stream, or from their burrows in the side of stream beds. The best time to search for them is at night with a torch; wade in the stream and net the koura as soon as you see them. There are two main species of saltwater crayfish: red crayfish and packhorse or green crayfish, the former being found from Three Kings to the Auckland Isles and the latter north of the Bay of Plenty. Crayfish contain little fat, but have a good protein content. The muscle fibres of the larger varieties, however, are not readily digested and some people are sensitive to the proteins of these creatures and develop a variety of allergic reactions after eating. All the same, there is no denying they have more flavour than most fish.

KOURA MAROKE (CRAYFISH TAILS)

Place the crayfish in cold water for long enough to enable you to remove the tail from the body without breaking it. Cut the shell from the flesh and hang it outside on a wire hook for two days to dry, making sure the tails are brought in each night. Now pound the tails flat, and rehang them on the line until the tails are completely dry. They are now ready to be stored in the larder. They are delicious to eat either as they are, or cooked with boiled meat and vegetables. It is possible to dry pipi, paua and kumara in the same way, except they are threaded onto string rather than hung on a hook.

Koura Mara

1 large crayfish
½ cup vinegar

1 Tblsp sugar, optional

Steep the crayfish in cold salted water for two or three days. Remove the crayfish from the brine and cut it into two lengthwise. Remove all the flesh and put into a bowl. Wash the shell carefully and dry well. Mix vinegar, sugar and ½ cup of water with the crayfish pulp. Pile back into the shells. Pipe mashed potato and mashed kumara around the shell and garnish with lemon and gherkin slices.

Crayfish Pie

60 g butter
2 Tblsp flour
½ tsp salt
300 ml milk
450 g cooked crayfish

1 Tblsp vinegar
1 tsp sugar
½ tsp mustard
Breadcrumbs

Melt the butter in a pot. Stir in flour and salt, add milk and cook for 3 minutes. Flake the fish and put in a casserole dish. Add vinegar, sugar, and mustard to the sauce. Pour over the fish and cover with breadcrumbs. Dot with butter and bake at 200°C for 25 minutes.

CRAYFISH NEWBURG

90 g butter

60 g onions, finely chopped

450 g crayfish, raw

1 Tblsp paprika

¼ cup dry sherry

1 tsp salt

Pinch white pepper

90 g flour

½ cup milk

½ cup cream

Melt butter and sauté onions until done; add raw chunks of crayfish. Sprinkle paprika over crayfish and stir gently to distribute paprika evenly. A high heat should be used. Pour in the dry sherry and simmer for approximately 3 minutes. Add salt, pepper and flour to the meat, stir gently. Slowly add combined hot milk and cream to the mixture, stir gently, bring to boil and simmer 3 minutes. Adjust consistency and seasoning. Serve with buttered rice.

Whitebait

WHITEBAIT FRITTERS

2 eggs
2 Tblsp self-raising flour
Salt and pepper
500 g whitebait

Beat eggs, flour and salt and pepper. Add whitebait. Cook in hot fat until golden brown. Serve immediately with lemon slices and parsley. Do not keep in oven or warming drawer as this will impair the flavour of the fritters.

WHITEBAIT OMELETTE (VERSION 1)

4 eggs
2 cups fresh whitebait
Pepper
1 Tblsp butter
$\frac{1}{2}$ tsp finely cut chives
$\frac{1}{2}$ tsp chopped parsley

Beat eggs well, add whitebait and pepper to taste. Melt butter in a frying pan, and when hot add the omelette. When cooked well, turn gently and serve, garnished with chives or parsley.

WHITEBAIT OMELETTE (VERSION 2)

2 eggs
$\frac{1}{2}$ tsp salt
3 Tblsp oil
1 cup whitebait

Beat eggs and salt together with a fork. Heat oil in a medium-size frying pan until hot. Pour in eggs. Reduce heat slightly and cook until the omelette is half set. While the top of the omelette is still liquid, carefully spread the whitebait over it. Continue to cook until the egg is almost set. Remove pan from heat and leave the omelette for a few minutes, then roll it and leave it with the join at the bottom until cold. Serve in 1.5 cm slices as a party supper dish.

Whitebait Puffs

250 g whitebait

2 eggs

1 Tblsp milk

2 Tblsp flour

1 tsp baking powder

1 tsp chopped parsley

Salt and pepper to taste

Mix all ingredients together, and fry in butter.

Whitebait Scramble

1 egg

1 Tblsp milk

Seasoning

1 cup whitebait

1 Tblsp butter

Beat egg and add milk and seasoning. Stir in whitebait until thoroughly coated in mixture. Melt butter in frying pan and add spoonfuls of mixture to pan and cook until the egg sets and both sides are lightly browned. More eggs per mixture can be used if desired. Makes about 12.

Tuna Heke

(Eels)

Two species of freshwater eels are found in New Zealand. They are the shortfin eel, the smaller of the species which seldom exceeds 1.0 m and weighs 4–5 kg, and the longfin eel, which may grow up to 1.8 m in length and weigh 40 kg or more. Both species can be found in swift-flowing water, but the shortfin prefers the slower-flowing muddy streams and coastal lakes, while the longfin can be found further inland.

Eels can be caught for most of the year, but each autumn (March–April), when the rivers are in flood, the eels migrate to the sea to spawn (generally at night), and thousands were formerly caught by the Maori, who built eel weirs in the rivers or dug blind channels into the shingle bars separating the lakes from the sea. Sometimes eels were speared, or caught on a line threaded with worms.

James Stack, son of one of the early New Zealand missionaries, was born in 1835 at a mission station in the Waikato district. Later the family moved to the East Cape, where James was the only white boy among scores of Maori children. He was eight when he had his first lesson in eeling:

'In the summer months the Maori were always poking about the banks of the river near our home at Waiapu, looking for eels. One day I asked a Maori boy to let me into the secrets of eel-fishing. He said he would do so.

'It was a very hot day. On reaching the river he told me to take off every stitch of clothing, and then to go feeling along the bank under the water until I found an opening into which I could push the whole length of my arm. If the hole was smooth, I was to pull out my arm and plug up the mouth of the opening.

'Then I was to search higher up for the other outlet of the eels' hiding place, which was generally a few feet away. When that was found, I was to push one arm up into the hole, while my free arm was to be used to break away the soil, so that I could push farther and farther in.

'I carefully watched the Maori boy do all this. As soon as he felt an eel, he slipped his finger and thumb along the body till they reached the gills. Then he quickly nipped his fingers together, pulled the eel out, and threw it up on the bank, where he killed it by beating the head with a stone or heavy piece of wood.

'I now began working along the bank and I was very much excited when I felt my first eel, which was almost two feet six inches long. I tried hard to hold it, but it kept slipping through my hands.

'As I raised it out of the water, I nearly lost it altogether. "Grip it with your teeth!" cried the Maori. I did as he said and though the tail smacked me about the face, I ran with my prize till I reached a dry shingle-bank, where I dropped it and killed it.

'By that time I found my mouth was full of nasty slime from off the creature's body, and though I washed my mouth again and again, I could not get rid of the horrid taste for a long time. After that I left my Maori friend to catch the eels when I found them.'

(Adapted from *Early Maoriland Adventures* of J. W. Stack.)

One of the most famous of New Zealand's explorers of the South Island,
Thomas Brunner, described the process of drying and skinning eels:

'If eels are carefully dried and skinned, the head cut off and opened down the belly, the bone carefully taken out and the flesh exposed to the smoke to dry, they would last some months and this is, in my opinion, the best way to eat them. An eel should be about 5–6 lb [2.5–3 kg] and, if too dry, soaking it in water for a few hours and then basting it over a slow fire, makes it a very good dish'

(Taylor, *Early Travellers in New Zealand*, 1959)

Joined leaves of the kanono or manono were wrapped around the bodies of eels which were being prepared for the hangi. The resulting food was greatly esteemed — eels cooked in this way are said to be a great delicacy. The eel has fine-textured flesh, good fat content and is excellent for cooking.

DRIED EELS

Clean the eels in the manner outlined by Brunner, ('silver bellies' are the best eels for drying), then grill over a hot fire, taking care not to cook them — they should only be half-cooked. String them on flax and hang out to dry in a strong wind. Do not leave the eels lying about for any length of time between the grilling and drying processes. Store in a dry and airy place. Do not let them go damp as they will go mouldy. When needed, steam them for 15 minutes and serve. Delicious with white sauce.

FRIED EEL

Skin and fillet an eel and cut into 5–8 cm lengths. Coat in seasoned flour, then in egg and bread-crumbs, and fry in hot fat until tender. Drain and serve with lemon.

BAKED EEL

Place a good sized eel, either sliced, filleted or whole, in a baking dish. Add three sliced onions, and cover with two thick slices of bacon. Place in a fairly hot oven and bake, pouring off the juice as it accumulates. When the eel looks half-cooked turn it over, moving the bacon to the bottom. Bake until cooked and golden brown, and serve with chips.

DELICIOUS EEL

Clean the eel by dipping it into very hot (but not boiling) water until it has a milky appearance. Wipe off all the slime. Remove the backbone, stomach and head, and open the eel out flat. Sprinkle liberally with salt and pepper and hang on a line in the sun to dry for 12–24 hours. Now it is ready to cook. Cut into pieces and place skin-side up in a pan. This allows fat to escape while cooking. Cook under a moderately hot grill for 15–20 minutes until the skin is crisp. Serve.

Tuna Natu (Mashed Eels and Kouka)

Boil puha, eel and kouka with onions until cooked. Remove from the stove, debone the eel and mash well with a fork. Add lard to the mixture, return to the stove and cook for another 10 minutes.

Eel with Parsley Sauce

Skin the eel and cut into 5–7 cm lengths. Put into cold, salted water; add a sprig of parsley and 1 or 2 slices of lemon. Simmer gently for 45 minutes then drain; serve with parsley sauce and garnish with lemon and parsley.

Stewed Eel

700 g eel

Salt

Lemon juice

¼ cup butter *or* margarine

Breadcrumbs

Cut the skinned eel in slices, clean and wash. Salt the slices and put in a casserole dish. Add a little water, lemon juice and butter. Sprinkle breadcrumbs over the fish, bake in a hot oven with the lid on for 15 or 20 minutes. Lower temperature, remove lid and cook for a further 10 minutes. Serve with boiled potatoes and a green salad.

JELLIED EEL (VERSION 1)

1 cup cooked eel
2 hard-boiled eggs, sliced
1 Tblsp gelatine
1 Tblsp vinegar

Flake the fish and place alternate layers of eel and sliced egg into a wet mould. Soak the gelatine in the vinegar, pour over 1 cup of boiling water and stir until clear. Add a little salt. When cool, pour carefully over the eel and egg and allow to set. Turn onto a dish, surround with lettuce leaves and serve with mayonnaise.

JELLIED EEL (VERSION 2)

Cut an eel into 5–7 cm lengths, having skinned it first. Put into cold water, adding a little salt and a squeeze of lemon juice. Use enough water to just cover the fish. Simmer very gently for 45–60 minutes until the fish is very tender. Lift out the eel and arrange in a mould or dish. Measure the liquid and, if a very firm jelly is required, add 1 tsp powdered gelatine to each 300 ml stock. Strain over the eels and allow to set. (If the liquid is boiled down (reduced), not only does it have a better flavour, but you can omit the gelatine.) A bay leaf or spice of your choice can be added for extra flavour.

Fish

BAKED FISH

With a sharp knife, make small cuts in the flesh of the fish. Place slivers of garlic, bacon or aromatic herbs into these cuts and lay the fish in a buttered fireproof dish. Pour over melted butter, oil or wine, and sprinkle with flour or breadcrumbs. Cook in a hot oven, covering the fish for part of the cooking time with greaseproof paper or aluminium foil to keep it moist. Baste regularly. Sprinkle the fish with salt, pepper and lemon juice, and serve with a sauce.

BRAISED FISH

Put a layer of sliced onions, carrots, white stems of leek, mushrooms, some bacon, thyme, parsley and bay leaf, fennel, salt and pepper into a casserole dish. Pour over a glass each of wine and water. Set the fish on the vegetables, cover and cook at a low temperature. When the fish is ready, serve with the vegetables. Strain the juices and reduce them, or thicken with beurre manie (1 Tblsp flour worked together with 1 Tblsp butter), egg yolks or cream.

FISH COOKED IN FOIL

Wash and trim the fish and, if desired, lightly grill or sauté it in butter. Place the fish on a sheet of aluminium foil or buttered greaseproof paper with some chopped onions and carrots, fresh or dried herbs, salt and pepper and a pinch of powdered mace or other appropriate seasoning. (Be careful not to overdo the flavouring as this is intensified by being sealed in.) Add butter and perhaps a spoonful of Pernod, white vermouth or sherry. A stuffing can also be added. Fold over the wrapping and seal the edges. Provided you have not pierced the wrapping, foil-wrapped food can be cooked directly over a low flame, on a flameproof mat over a fire, or in the oven. (Food wrapped in greaseproof paper can only be cooked in the oven.) Cook until the fish is tender, and serve hot.

BLUE COD

BAKED BLUE COD

450 g blue cod fillets

Salt

1 slice lemon

1 Tblsp vinegar

1 Tblsp flour

1 Tblsp dry mustard

1 tsp sugar

½ tsp salt

1 egg yolk

¾ cup milk

1 Tblsp butter

Sprinkle the blue cod with salt and top with a lemon slice, then wrap in foil. Bake 20–25 minutes at 175°C.

Meanwhile, prepare the Hollandaise sauce. Mix vinegar, flour, mustard, sugar and salt to a smooth paste. Beat egg yolk, add milk and stir into the mustard mixture. Bring to the boil, stirring constantly. Simmer 2 minutes. Add the butter and mix thoroughly. Keep the lid on the saucepan until sauce is required. Serve the fish with Hollandaise sauce, carrot sticks and baked potatoes.

If blue cod is not available this dish can be made with terakihi, red cod, butterfish or gurnard.

Blue Cod with Almonds

450 g boneless blue cod fillets	Butter
¼ cup milk	60 g butter, extra
½ tsp salt	60 g chopped almonds
Flour	1 tsp tarragon, optional

Wipe the fish, dip it in milk to which salt has been added, then coat with flour. Fry in hot butter until golden on both sides, approximately 6–7 minutes. Remove the fish, add the extra butter to the pan, add the almonds, and cook until light brown.

Arrange the fish on a hot serving dish and pour over the almonds and the butter in which they were cooked. Sprinkle with tarragon leaves if desired, and garnish with lemon wedges, oval shaped potatoes, and black grapes or olives.

If blue cod is not available this dish can also be made with terakihi, flounder, sole or butterfish.

Spicy Fried Blue Cod

2 Tblsp flour	60 g butter
½ tsp nutmeg	1 Tblsp butter, extra
½ tsp salt	1 Tblsp flour, extra
Pepper	¼ tsp nutmeg, extra
4 blue cod fillets	¾ cup milk

Combine flour, nutmeg, salt and pepper then use to coat the fish. Melt the butter in a frypan, add the fish and cook for 6–8 minutes, turning once. In a separate pan, melt the extra butter, stir in the extra flour and nutmeg, and cook for 1 minute. Slowly add the milk and cook until sauce thickens, stirring constantly. Serve the fish and sauce together, garnished with lemon wedges, and accompanied by mushrooms, cucumber, tomato, potatoes and a green salad.

If blue cod is not available this dish can be made with terakihi, snapper, hake or gurnard.

STEWART ISLAND BLUE COD

450 g blue cod fillets	1 tsp cornflour
6 oysters and their juice	12 black grapes, halved
½ cup cream *or* top milk	and seeds removed
Salt and pepper	

Cut fish into 2 cm cubes and poach in the oyster juice, adding a little water if required. When fish is tender, remove to a hot serving dish. Add the cream to the liquid in which the fish was cooked, season with salt and pepper and heat. Mix cornflour to a smooth paste with a little extra milk and use to thicken the sauce. Boil 1 minute then add the roughly chopped oysters. Cook 2 minutes. Pour the sauce over the fish and garnish with grapes. (If grapes are not available use prunes or tomatoes.) Serve with crescent-shaped puff pastries and vegetables.

If blue cod is not available this dish can be made with flounder, sole or John Dory.

Flounder and Sole

Asparagus and Flounder Rolls

8 fillets flounder *or* sole

8 spears asparagus (tinned, or cooked in
    water and butter)

Butter

Sprinkle fillets lightly with salt. Place a spear of asparagus and a dot of butter on each fillet, roll up and secure with a toothpick. Place under a preheated grill and baste with butter. Cook for approximately 7 minutes, basting as necessary and turning once. Serve with vegetables and creamed potato.

Flounder or Sole Lenore

4 medium flounder *or* sole	Butter, melted
Fresh lemon juice	8 button mushrooms
Salt and pepper	250 g tin creamed mushrooms
Flour	Parsley, finely chopped
	Paprika

Remove heads, fins and skin from fish, sprinkle with lemon juice then salt and pepper. Dip first in flour then melted butter. Place under a preheated grill with the button mushrooms and cook until the flesh is just tender (approximately 4 minutes each side),

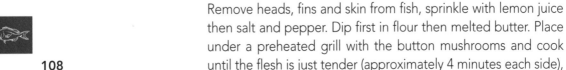

and the mushrooms are done. Remove the bones by making a cut along the backbone and folding the fish towards the sides like the pages of an open book. Break the backbone 1.5 cm from the tail and lift the skeleton out, taking care not to break it or damage the fish. Fill the cavity with hot creamed mushrooms. Arrange the fish on a serving plate and keep it in a warm oven until required.

Using kitchen scissors trim the bones to an oval shape. Dip one side of the skeleton in parsley and the other in paprika. Bend to form a slight arch and place on the fish in that position. Garnish with the grilled mushrooms and lemon wedges. Serve with puff pastry crescents.

SOLE BONNE FEMME

4 flounder *or* sole fillets	**Parsley, finely chopped**
Seasoned flour	**2 tomatoes, chopped**
Butter	**Grated cheese**
8 mushrooms	

Coat the fish with seasoned flour, and fry in the butter. Remove from pan and arrange on hot serving plate. Chop the mushrooms and fry in the remaining hot butter, then sprinkle with the parsley. Arrange around the fillets, adding chopped tomatoes sprinkled with cheese for extra colour. Garnish with lemon slices topped with olives if desired. Serve with vegetables and buttered potatoes.

If flounder or sole is not available this dish can be made with John Dory or blue cod.

STUFFED FLOUNDER

4 small flounder *or* **sole**

Salt

¾ cup crushed pineapple, drained

¼ cup finely chopped celery

60 g butter

Remove fins from fish but leave the head on. Bone the fish as follows: on the underside make a cut along the backbone; with a small sharp knife, separate the fillet from the bones; using scissors, break the backbone near the head and 1 cm from the tail, then cut around the sides of the skeleton and lift out the bones. Sprinkle the cavity with a little salt then stuff with the combined pineapple and celery. Close the pocket and secure with toothpicks.

Melt the butter in a roasting pan, add the fish and bake at 175°C for 20–25 minutes or until tender when tested with a fork. Garnish with lemon wedges and tomatoes. Serve with baked potatoes and vegetables or salad.

Garfish

Fried Garfish with Tartare Sauce

4 portions garfish

Flour

Pepper and salt

1 tsp gherkin, chopped

1 tsp parsley

1 tsp capers

½ tsp tarragon

¼ tsp sugar

150 ml mayonnaise

Cut off the heads and tails of the fish. Wash garfish well in fresh water and dry thoroughly on absorbent paper. Coat fish with plain flour seasoned with pepper and shake off any excess. Deep-fry in hot oil until cooked and golden brown in colour. Dust with a little salt just before serving. Serve with tartare sauce made by combining gherkin, parsley, capers, tarragon, sugar and mayonnaise together with salt and pepper to taste.

GROPER

BAKED GROPER FILLETS

½ cup dried breadcrumbs

½ cup milk

¼ tsp pepper

½ tsp salt

700 g groper cutlets

½ cup salad oil

2 Tblsp lemon juice

¼ tsp pepper, extra

1 Tblsp salt, extra

Spread breadcrumbs on greaseproof paper. Mix milk and seasonings. Dip fish in milk then coat with crumbs. Place in greased ovenproof dish. Combine oil, lemon juice, and extra salt and pepper in a stoppered bottle, and shake thoroughly. Pour over cutlets. Bake at 250°C in the middle of the oven for 20–30 minutes or until golden brown and tender. Serve with baked tomatoes, green vegetables and chips.

GROPER KEBABS

500 g groper fillets

1 small tin pineapple chunks

4 cocktail onions

Salt

30 g butter

30 ml pineapple syrup

Pre-heat grill. Cut fish into chunks, approximately 2–3 cm square. Arrange fish and pineapple alternately on skewers, finishing with a cocktail onion. Sprinkle with salt. Place kebabs on grill rack. Melt butter, add pineapple syrup, then pour half this liquid over the kebabs. Grill kebabs 7–8 minutes, turn, pour over remaining butter and pineapple liquid, then grill until fish is tender. Serve with fried noodles.

If groper is not available this dish can be made with terakihi.

Perky Groper Casserole

1 medium onion, finely chopped

120 g tasty cheese, grated

4 groper cutlets

$\frac{1}{2}$ cup milk

1 tsp salt

$\frac{1}{2}$ tsp pepper

$\frac{1}{2}$ tsp dry mustard

$\frac{1}{2}$ tsp Worcestershire sauce

Combine onion and half the cheese and spread over the bottom of a casserole dish. Place fish on top. Cover with remaining cheese. Combine milk, salt, pepper, mustard and Worcestershire sauce then pour over fish. Bake at 210°C for 25–30 minutes. Serve with baked potatoes and salad.

If groper is not available this dish can be made with snapper.

Groper in Sweet and Sour Sauce

180 g long grain rice

500 g groper fillets

1 small egg, beaten

½ cup cornflour, seasoned
   with salt and pepper

30 g butter

2 slices root ginger, finely chopped

1 Tblsp cornflour

1 Tblsp brown sugar

2 Tblsp white vinegar

¾ cup fish stock *or* water

Boil rice according to instructions. Cut fish into bite-size pieces, dip first in egg then in seasoned cornflour. Melt butter in heavy-based frypan. Add fish and root ginger. Cook until golden and tender, turning several times. Blend cornflour, brown sugar, vinegar and fish stock. Add to fish, bring to the boil and cook 4–5 minutes. Serve on boiled rice and garnish with lemon and parsley.

If groper is not available this dish can be made with hake, snapper or moki.

Gurnard

Baked Stuffed Gurnard

1 whole gurnard

1 tsp salt

1 small onion, finely chopped

30 g butter, melted

1 cup soft breadcrumbs

1 tsp finely chopped mint

1 Tblsp finely chopped parsley

60 g butter, extra

3 rashers fat bacon

1 cup pineapple juice

1 Tblsp cornflour

Using scissors remove fins from gurnard. Wipe fish then sprinkle with salt. Combine onion, melted butter, breadcrumbs, mint and parsley to make a stuffing. Stuff the fish and skewer or sew up the opening. Melt the extra butter in a baking dish and add the stuffed fish. Cover with bacon rashers and baste well. Bake at 180°C for 35–40 minutes or until fish is tender when tested with a fork. Remove fish to a hot serving plate. Drain off any excess fat from baking dish and add pineapple juice. Mix cornflour to a smooth paste with a little water and use to thicken the gravy. Serve sauce with baked gurnard.

Savoury Gurnard Rolls

4 small fillets gurnard
Salt and pepper
125 g sausage meat
Butter *or* oil

Sprinkle fillets with a little salt and pepper. Spread with sausage meat, roll up each fillet and secure with toothpicks. Fry in butter or oil. Serve with vegetables or salad.

Slim Jack

500 g gurnard fillets
½ cup top milk
1 tsp salt
1 small onion, cut in rings
1 bay leaf
2 tomatoes

Remove any bones from fish and cut into 2 cm cubes. Grease the top of a double boiler and place the fish in it. Add top milk, salt, onion rings and bay leaf. Cook over boiling water for 20 minutes. Cut tomatoes into wedges, add to fish and heat through for 5–10 minutes. Remove bay leaf, spoon sauce over fish cubes and serve.

KINGFISH

MARINADE FOR KINGFISH STEAKS

¼ cup soy sauce

¼ cup tomato pulp

¼ cup orange juice

2 Tblsp lemon juice

1 clove garlic, crushed

1 tsp oregano

½ tsp salt

¼ tsp black pepper

To make the marinade, simply mix all the ingredients together. Leave fish in marinade for about two hours, turning occasionally. Barbecue or grill steaks, brushing with the marinade from time to time.

MANGO

One of the principal saltwater fish which was formerly eaten was the shark (mango), which was hooked in great numbers. Strictly speaking mango were dogfish of the *Mustelus* and *Squalus* genus. The fish were cut open and hung up in the sun and wind on high horizontal poles to dry for 4–5 months. Their ova was preserved by drying, and was considered a great delicacy. Mango was a winter food, a small quantity being cooked as a relish for kumara.

ATE MANGO (SHARK'S LIVER)

Take the liver from a fresh shark or dogfish. Be careful to remove the gall bladder without breaking it. Wrap the liver in clean cabbage leaves and steam for 1 hour. This can be eaten with any boiled fish.

MANGO MAROKE (CURED OR DRIED SHARK)
(VERSION 1)

Cut fresh shark into strips, hang out to dry and store for winter use. When required, cut the dried shark into 10 cm pieces, place on top of kumara and steam for 30 minutes.

MANGO MAROKE (VERSION 2)

Place one whole dehydrated fish into a good fire, and leave until well charred and burnt black. Remove the blackened fish from the fire and when it is slightly cool, scrape away all the charred shark skin with a strong knife. Immediately below the skin you will find golden flesh which is ready for eating. To remove the flesh break the fish lengthwise. A powerful odour will be emitted, and this can be disconcerting at first, but the flesh itself is very tasty. This is a good side dish, but only small portions can be eaten at a time.

MULLET

STUFFED MULLET

1 whole mullet
Salt and pepper
1 cup dry breadcrumbs, white
1 bunch spring onions
1 cup chopped oysters
2 knobs butter

Wipe fish dry and sprinkle it inside with salt and pepper. Mix breadcrumbs with chopped spring onions, oysters, salt and pepper to taste, and add sufficient butter to bind it all together. Stuff the fish and place on buttered foil, wrapping it securely. Bake in a baking dish at 175°C for 35–40 minutes. Remove the foil, and serve the fish garnished with lemon wedges and sprigs of parsley. This dish is ideal to barbecue.

Snapper

Baked Snapper

    1.5 kg snapper

    Seasoned flour

    1 egg, beaten

    Dry breadcrumbs

    1 cup milk

    1 bay leaf

    1 tsp mace

    Salt and pepper

    1 Tblsp flour

If using a whole fish, remove the head or use tail section of a larger fish. Wipe fish then dip first in seasoned flour, then in beaten egg, and finally in breadcrumbs. Place fish in greased ovenware dish or roasting pan. Bake at 175°C for approximately 30 minutes, or until tender when tested with a fork, turning once during cooking.

In a saucepan, heat the milk with the bay leaf, mace, and salt and pepper. Remove the cooked fish and place on a serving dish. Add the flour to the stock remaining in the baking dish and cook for 1 minute over a direct heat. Gradually add the infused milk and cook for 3 minutes, stirring constantly. Serve the sauce with the baked fish.

Chilled Snapper

6 snapper steaks

Salt

¼ cup salad oil

2 medium onions, diced

4 tomatoes, roughly chopped

1 green chilli *or* green pepper

60 g bacon, chopped

1 clove garlic, crushed

1 Tblsp brown sugar

1 tsp paprika

1 stalk celery, chopped

¼ cup white wine

Salt and pepper

1 tsp chopped parsley

Wipe snapper steaks and sprinkle thoroughly with salt; place in a casserole dish. Heat oil in pan and add onion, tomatoes, chilli or green pepper, bacon, garlic, brown sugar, paprika and celery. Simmer together until thick and pulpy. Add wine, and cook a further 2 minutes. Season to taste. Pour this tomato mixture around the fish. Cover with a fitting lid or foil, and bake at 175°C for 30 minutes. Chill thoroughly and sprinkle with parsley before serving.

DEEP-FRIED SNAPPER FILLETS

4 medium snapper fillets

2 Tblsp flour

½ tsp salt

¼ tsp pepper

1 small egg

Dried breadcrumbs

Fat *or* oil for frying

Parsley

Wipe snapper fillets. Mix flour with salt and pepper. Lightly beat egg and season. Coat the snapper fillets in flour, then dip in egg and finally in breadcrumbs. Deep fry in fat at 160°C. Just before fish is cooked place a bunch of washed and dried parsley in hot fat. Cook fish and parsley together for 1 minute. Serve garnished with either fried parsley or lemon slices decorated with raw chopped parsley and paprika.

Red Snapper Fried with a Better Beer Batter

1 cup self-raising flour
1/4 tsp salt
1/4 tsp paprika
Freshly ground white peppercorns
1 egg, separated
2 Tblsp soy bean oil
1 cup beer
Red snapper fillets

Sift flour, salt, paprika, and a pinch of pepper into a bowl. Add egg yolk and soy bean oil. Stir into flour and gradually add beer, stirring until the batter is free of lumps. Do not overbeat as this will cause the mixture to blister when cooked. Beat the egg white until firm, fold into batter mixture. Dip fish pieces in to batter and deep fry in hot fat or oil until golden brown. Serve with shaped tomato pieces, cheese, parsley and lemon wedges. The beer gives this batter a tasty, spicy and aromatic flavour, making it quite morish and different from an ordinary batter.

SNAPPER PIQUANTE

450 g snapper fillets

125 ml milk

90 ml dry white wine

½ tsp nutmeg

1 tsp salt

Pepper to taste

1 clove garlic, crushed

30 g butter

2 onions

4 tomatoes

Parsley

Place snapper fillets in ovenproof dish, add milk, wine, nutmeg, salt and pepper, and crushed garlic. Bake at 170°C for 20–25 minutes.

Melt butter in saucepan. Slice onions into rings 0.5 cm thick and sauté in butter until tender, but not too brown. Cut each tomato into eight pieces, add to onion and heat. Season with extra salt and pepper. Place onion and tomato mixture on hot serving dish. Remove fish from liquid and place on top of onion and tomatoes. Garnish with parsley.

Terakihi

Grilled Terakihi

300 ml milk	20 g butter
1 small onion	2 Tblsp flour
2 cloves	Pinch nutmeg
Bouquet garni	Pinch cayenne
2 peppercorns	Salt
1 small bay leaf	4 fillets terakihi
1 blade mace	Melted butter

First make the béchamel sauce. Put milk in saucepan with onion into which cloves have been stuck, add bouquet garni, peppercorns, bay leaf and mace. Bring slowly to boiling point and simmer 5 minutes. Strain. In a separate pan, melt butter, add flour and cook gently for 2–3 minutes, but do not brown. Add seasoned milk gradually and stir until boiling. Simmer 4–5 minutes. Add nutmeg, cayenne and salt to taste. Keep warm while you cook the fish.

Wipe terakihi fillets then sprinkle with salt. Brush with melted butter. Place under a hot grill. Turn once during cooking, brushing each side with a mixture of equal quantities of melted butter and hot water. The fish is cooked when it flakes when tested with a fork. Serve with béchamel sauce and vegetables.

Simple Terakihi Cru

450 g terakihi fillets

2 spring onions, finely chopped

Juice of 3 lemons, strained

60 g cucumber, diced

60 g celery, diced

60 g carrots, diced

120 g sweetened condensed milk

1½ tsp salt

½ tsp dry mustard

2 Tblsp plain yoghurt *or* ¼ cup top milk

¼ cup lemon juice, extra

Pepper

Shredded lettuce

Cut fish into 1 cm cubes. Place in casserole dish with spring onion and add lemon juice. Cover and leave in fridge for 12 hours or at room temperature for 4 hours. Strain off lemon juice and mix in cucumber, celery and carrot. Make a dressing by combining the condensed milk with the salt, mustard, yoghurt or milk, extra lemon juice and pepper to taste. Allow to stand for 10 minutes then add to the fish salad and serve on a bed of shredded lettuce.

KERIKERI TERAKIHI

1 large orange
450 g terakihi fillets
Salt
1 egg
60 g peanuts, chopped
Butter *or* oil

Peel orange and slice fairly thickly. Rub fish with one slice of orange. Sprinkle fillets with salt. Dip fish in beaten egg then in chopped nuts, using a knife blade to press nuts firmly into fish. Fry with a slice of orange on each fillet. Turn once during cooking, returning orange to top of fillets. Serve with salad made with cabbage, apple, tomato and chopped orange.

Terakihi Mornay

1 Tblsp white vinegar

1 tsp salt

1 small fillet per person

30 g butter

1 tsp salt, extra

$\frac{1}{2}$ tsp cayenne pepper

3 Tblsp flour

$\frac{3}{4}$ cup milk

1 Tblsp lemon juice

2 gherkins, sliced

1 Tblsp mayonnaise

60 g grated medium tasty cheese *or* cream cheese

Breadcrumbs

15 g parmesan cheese

Combine 2 cups of water, white vinegar and salt; poach fish in this until cooked; remove fish and reserve stock. In a separate pan melt butter, add extra salt, cayenne pepper and flour. Add milk gradually, stir until thick and flour is cooked. Remove from heat and add lemon juice, gherkins, mayonnaise, tasty or cream cheese. Place fish in an ovenproof dish and pour over the sauce. Cover with dry breadcrumbs and parmesan cheese. Bake at 175°C for 10 minutes to heat the dish through and brown the breadcrumbs. Serve with baked tomatoes and baked potatoes or toast fingers.

TROUT

TAUPO TROUT

½ green pepper
1 Tblsp butter
1 cup cooked rice
1 onion, chopped
Slice of bacon, chopped, extra
½ cup grated tasty cheese
Salt and ground pepper
1 trout, cleaned
7 rashers bacon

Cook the green pepper in the butter for 1 minute. Add the rice, onion, extra bacon, cheese and seasonings. Use this mixture to stuff the trout, then wrap it in bacon slices, season well with ground pepper and put three or four knobs of butter along the top of the trout. Wrap the fish in tin foil and seal. Place in a heated oven at 200°C for 1 hour. Serve with lemon juice.

TROUT AMANDINE

4–6 fresh trout
Salt and freshly ground black pepper
Milk
Flour
1 Tblsp olive oil

120 g butter

4–6 tblsp blanched slivered almonds

Juice of half a lemon

2–4 Tblsp finely chopped parsley

Season cleaned trout with salt and a little pepper, dip them first in milk, then in flour, and sauté for 30 minutes in the oil and half the butter until golden brown on both sides. Drain the used fat from the pan and melt the remaining butter. Add the almonds and cook, shaking pan continuously, until the almonds are golden brown. Add lemon juice and parsley and pour the sauce over trout on a heated platter.

TROUT PÈRE LOUIS

4 Tblsp butter

4 fresh trout

6–8 Tblsp cream

2 Tblsp Grand Marnier

2 Tblsp cognac

Salt and freshly ground black pepper

2–4 Tblsp sliced almonds, toasted

Melt butter in a thick-bottomed frying pan and sauté trout until tender. Heat cream in a saucepan without letting it come to the boil. Stir in Grand Marnier and cognac and add salt and freshly ground black pepper to taste. Place trout on a heated serving dish; pour over the sauce and sprinkle with sliced toasted almonds. Serve immediately.

Truite Marinée Étoile

6 medium sized trout

6 Tblsp olive oil

Malt vinegar

Marjoram

Salt and freshly ground black pepper

120 g baby onions

Vinegar, extra

Escoffier's Sauce Diable

Chilli sauce

Clean and trim trout and sauté gently in olive oil until fish flakes with a fork. Place trout in a porcelain bowl and allow to cool.

Combine enough malt vinegar to cover trout with marjoram, and salt and pepper to taste, and bring to the boil. Pour marinade mixture over the trout and allow to marinate for 24 hours. Boil the baby onions until just cooked, then marinate them in the extra vinegar.

Place trout on a serving dish. Add a little Sauce Diable and chilli sauce to the marinade, and pour this over the trout. Serve with the pickled baby onions.

Index

Asparagus and Flounder
    Rolls 108
Ate Mango 118

Baked Blue Cod 105
Baked Eel 100
Baked Fish 103
Baked Groper Fillets 112
Baked Kina 50
Baked Scallops 77
Baked Snapper 121
Baked Stuffed Gurnard 115
Barbecued Paua with Onions
    62
Basic Poached Scallops 77
Blue cod
    baked 105
    spicy fried 106
    Stewart Island 107
    with almonds 106
Braised Fish 104
Bread
    camp-oven 12
    paraoa koa 14
    paraoa parai 13
    paraoa takakau 11
    pua 17
    raupo 15–17
    rewena 13
    takakau 12

Cabbage tree 20
Cake
    pumpkin 33

Casseroles
    paua 70
    perky groper 113
    pork, apple and kumara
      28
Camp-Oven Bread 12
Candied Kumara 27
Chilled Snapper 122
Cockles
    collection of 49
    fritters 75
    preserved 75
Cold Weather Kuku 52
Corn 34–37
Corned Beef, Puha and
    Kouka 40
Crayfish *see also koura*
    collection of 91
    newburg 93
    pie 92
    tails 91
Creamed Paua 68
Creamed Paua and Bacon 69
Creme Paua 62
Cured Shark 118, 119
Curried Scallops 78

Deep-Fried Mussels
    Béarnaise 55
Deep-Fried Snapper Fillets
    123
Delicious Eel 100
Dips
    mussel 52

savoury, with minced paua
    67
Dried Eels 99
Dried Kaanga Wai 35
Dried Shark 118, 119

Eel *see also tuna heke*
    baked 100
    delicious 100
    dried 99
    fried 100
    jellied 102
    stewed 101
    with parsley sauce 101

Favourite Brown Stew With
    Kumara Topping 30
Fish
    baked 103
    braised 104
    cooked in foil 104
Flounder
    lenore 108
    rolls, asparagus and 108
    stuffed 110
Fried Bread 13
Fried Eel 100
Fried Garfish with Tartare
    Sauce 111
Fried Mussels 54
Fried Paua 62
Fried Scallops 81
Fritters
    cockle 75

133

paua 65–66
toheroa 86
whitebait 94

Garfish
fried, with tartare sauce
111
Golden Tuangi Batter Balls
89
Grilled Scallops 80
Grilled Terakihi 126
Groper
casserole, perky 113
fillets, baked 112
in sweet and sour sauce
114
kebabs 112
Gurnard
baked stuffed 115
rolls, savoury 116
slim jack 116

Hangi
oven 10
traditional 1–9
Hinau 17–18

Jellied Eel 102

Kaanga
pudding, scraped 36
pungarehu 37
roroi 37
wai 35
wai custard 36
wai, dried 35
waru 36
Kakahi soup 57
Kao 24

Karaka 18
Karengo 22
Kerikeri Terakihi 128
Kina
baked 50
collection of 49
soup 50
Kingfish
steaks, marinade for 117
Kouka 20
with corned beef and
puha 40
Koura see also crayfish
mara 92
maroke 91
Kuku see also mussels
cold weather 52
Kumara
and apricots 27
candied 27
casserole, pork, apple and
28
chowder 26
crumbed roll 28
kao 24
kotero 25
loaf 29
oriental rissoles 29
pie 25
roroi 31
sweet potato poi 31
topping, favourite brown
stew with 30

Maize With Wood Ash 34
Makaue 22
Mango
ate 118
maroke 118, 119

Marinade for Kingfish Steaks
117
Mullet
stuffed 120
Mussels see also kuku
and puha 39
béarnaise, deep-fried 55
collection of 49
dip 52
freshwater 57
fried 54
in batter 53
pie 56
preserved 51
scalloped 56
soup 51
Mutton bird
supreme 44
to cook 43

Omelette
whitebait 95
Oriental Kumara Rissoles 29
Oysters
collection of 49
rockefeller 59
sauce 58
soup 58
stew 60

Pakeke 32
Paraoa Koa 14
Paraoa Parai 13
Paraoa Takakau 11
Parengo 22–23
Paua
and meat pie 71
barbecued, with onions 62
casserole 70

134

collection of 49, 61
creamed 68
creamed, and bacon 69
creme 62
fried 62
fritters 65, 66
in cream 69
minced, and savoury dip
  67
pancakes 67
pickled 68
self-pressure cooked 61
soup 64
steaks 63
to freeze 61
with pineapple sauce
  70
Perky Groper Casserole
  113
Pickled Paua 68
Pies
  crayfish 92
  kumara 25
  mussel 56
  paua and meat 71
Pipi
  and curry stew 72
  appetisers 72
  collection of 49
  luncheon dish 74
  soup 73
Poached Scallops 76
Poaka Tahu 46
Pork
  apple and kumara
    casserole 28
  poaka tahu 46
  preserved 46
  tao mana 47

Potato
  pakeke 32
  soup 32
Preserved Cockles 75
Preserved Mussels 51
Preserved Pork 46
Pua 17
Puha
  and mussels 39
  mara 39
  penupenu 38
  tiotio 38
  toroi 39
  with corned beef and
    kouka 40
Pukeko Stew 45
Pukou 21
Pumpkin
  cake 33
  soup 33
Pupu see cockles

Raupo 15–17
Rauriki see puha
Red Snapper Fried with a
  Better Beer Batter 124
Rewena 13
Rimurapa 23
Rissoles
  oriental kumara 29
Roroi 31

Salad
  scallop 79
  ti-tree 20
  watercress 42
Savoury Dip and Minced
  Paua 67
Savoury Gurnard Rolls 116

Scalloped Mussels 56
Scallops
  and mushrooms in white
    wine 83
  baked 77
  basic poached 77
  collection of 49
  curried 78
  fried 81
  grilled 80
  in jackets 79
  kebabs 80
  mornay 82
  poached 76
  salad 79
Scraped Kaanga Pudding 36
Sea Lettuce Hash 23
Self-Pressure Cooked Paua
  61
Shark see mango
Shark's Liver 118
Shellfish
  collection of 48–49
Simple Terakihi Cru 127
Slim Jack 116
Snapper
  baked 121
  chilled 122
  fillets, deep-fried 123
  piquante 125
  red, fried with a better
    beer batter 124
Sole
  bonne femme 109
  lenore 108
Sooty shearwater 43
Soup
  kakahi 57
  kina 50

kumara 26
mussel 51
oyster 58
paua 64
pipi 73
potato 32
pumpkin 33
toheroa 85, 86
watercress 41
Spicy Fried Blue Cod 106
Steamed Toheroa 84
Steamed Tuangi 88
Stew
   favourite brown stew with
     kumara topping 30
   oyster 60
   pipi and curry 72
   pukeko 45
Stewart Island Blue Cod
   107
Stewed Eel 101
Stuffed Flounder 110
Stuffed Mullet 120
Swamp hen *see pukeko*

Sweet Potato Poi 31

Takakau 12
Tao Mana 47
Taupo Trout 130
Terakihi
   cru, simple 127
   grilled 126
   Kerikeri 128
   mornay 129
Titi 43
Ti tree 20
   salad 20
Toheroa
   chowder 86
   collection of 49, 84
   fritters 86
   patties 87
   soup 85
   steamed 84
   to prepare 84
Toretore *see kina*
Trout
   amandine 130

pere louis 131
Taupo 130
truite marinée étoile 132
Truite Marinée Étoile 132
Tuangi
   batter balls, golden 89
   steamed 88
   to clean 88
Tuatua, collection of 49
Tuna heke *see also eel*
   natu 101
Tupakihi 21
Tutu 21

Watercress
   salad 42
   soup 41
   toroi 41
Whanake 20
Whitebait
   fritters 94
   omelette 95
   puffs 96
   scramble 96